D1084672

Illustrious
Evidence

PUBLISHED UNDER THE AUSPICES OF THE

WILLIAM ANDREWS CLARK MEMORIAL LIBRARY

UNIVERSITY OF CALIFORNIA, LOS ANGELES

Illustrious Evidence

Approaches to English Literature of the Early Seventeenth Century

Edited, with an Introduction, by
EARL MINER

1975
UNIVRESITY OF CALIFORNIA PRESS
BERKELEY · LOS ANGELES · LONDON

University of California Press
Berkeley and Los Angeles, California
University of California Press, Ltd.
London, England

For
Robert S. Vosper and
William E. Conway

CONTENTS

PREFACE

The six essays making up this book were delivered in similar form as papers before an audience of students and faculty at UCLA during my tenure as Clark Library Professor in 1971–72. Each was given on a Thursday afternoon, and each was followed by discussion in the Baroque drawing room of the Clark Library and subsequently over coffee. Three papers besides the half dozen given here were also presented, but they have been reserved as being designed for separate publication or as falling outside a definable volume. Since the three speakers who do not contribute to this volume are highly respected scholars and, above all, personal friends, I wish to thank them by the expedient of mentioning their names and topics. French Fogle spoke about definitions of pastoral from the Greeks to the Renaissance; William Frost spoke about the lines of literary development leading to Samuel Richardson; and John Wallace discussed Denham's *Cooper's Hill*. I am grateful to each of these people for stimulating their audiences to lively discussion and for their kindness to me in participating in the activities of my year as Clark Professor.

The six papers remaining seem to me exemplary discussions of fundamental scholarly and critical matters, and I have more to say of them in the Introduction following. I do not know what might be a sufficiently conspicuous place to make clear my gratitude to the Clark Library Committee for my appointment, to the

Clark Library staff for its unsurpassed kind assistance, or to the faculty and students who made the occasions of these papers so exciting. It was the happiest, although in one way also the saddest, of the seventeen happy years that my wife and I enjoyed at UCLA. Of the prospect of introducing such speakers and of spending a year's quiet work in the Clark Library, any of us would ask with Virgil's Mopsus whether anything could give us greater happiness than this? In retrospect the year appears a bit more georgic than that but altogether satisfying. I hope that the papers presented here provide a wider audience with something of the thought and pleasure they first gave in southern California.

ACKNOWLEDGMENTS

After my thanks to the Clark Library, I must express my gratitude to the Central Stenographic Bureau at UCLA for the typing of this last in a series of manuscripts starting in 1957. The Research Committee at Princeton has also given me aid in the final preparation of the manuscript. And at the end of a chronology of indebtedness, I want to thank Jennifer Brady for her vigilant assistance on the index. From Herbert's *Proverbs:* "Good service is great inchantment."

E. M.

Princeton
Winter, 1973

CONTRIBUTORS

Robert M. Adams is Professor of English at the University of California, Los Angeles. His essay on Chaos in *Paradise Lost* brings him back to an author and a poem treated in his widely read *Ikon* or *Milton and the Modern Critics* (to use both titles). He has also concerned himself with modern literature, especially Joyce, and with translation, which he has himself practiced in rendering writers like Stendahl.

Stanley E. Fish is Professor of English at the Johns Hopkins University. His essay on *Comus* represents an example and a refinement of the kind of interpretation that made his study of *Paradise Lost—Surprised by Sin*—seem fresh to so many readers. His most recent book is *Self-Consuming Artifacts: The Experience of Seventeenth-Century Literature*, and he is at work on a monograph dealing with George Herbert.

Frank L. Huntley is Professor Emeritus of the University of Michigan. His scholarly career began with studies of Dryden's criticism and subsequently worked back through the major prose writers of the century. He is well known for his studies and editions of Sir Thomas Browne and Jeremy Taylor. And recently he has been examining the poet and divine, Joseph Hall.

Barbara K. Lewalski is Professor of English at Brown University. Her two major books are *Milton's Brief Epic* on *Paradise Regained* and Donne's *Anniversaries and the Poetry of Praise*. In these she shows how particular poets make use of the major ideas of their times. She is presently engaged in a study of "biblical poetics," to show how religious poetry was related to ideas about the literary books of the Bible.

Louis L. Martz is Professor of English at Yale University and Director of the Beinecke Library. Although he has long been interested in modern poetry, a subject he has taught and written about, and although he is an editor of the edition of Sir Thomas More, he is best known for his books on seventeenth-century poetry. In particular, *The Poetry of Meditation* opened the study of the religious poetry of the century to a new understanding and has inspired many subsequent studies.

James Thorpe is Director of the Henry E. Huntington Library and Art Gallery. Among his published works is an edition of the poems of Sir George Etherege. He has written about the nature of scholarly study of English literature. His *Principles of Textual Criticism* has been widely praised for its unusual common sense and literary sensitivity in discussing the difficult art of editing literary texts.

The editor of this volume, Earl Miner, is Professor of English at Princeton University and has recently completed a three-volume study of seventeenth-century English poetry.

INTRODUCTION

Earl Miner

Study of the literature of the seventeenth century in England
differs not a great deal from literary study of other periods or
countries. Certain central questions recur, and the varieties of
useful answers hitherto discovered are not numerous. In some respects, the essays in this book pose questions, and devise means
for answer, that ought to seem familiar to a medievalist or to a
student of contemporary literature. In other respects, however,
seventeenth-century English literature is quite its own thing. On
the one hand, it possesses extraordinary variety and quality. On
the other hand, what would it be like to live in the last century in
which the novel did not exist? What would it be like to live in
what has been called the most unstable period of modern British
history? Or to know with certainty that the best classical scholars
lived across the water, and that the prestige of the culture of another country under the Sun King exceeded that of one's own literature? What would it be like to have no literary history of
English, no full-length critical study of an English author, and
no large library in which to study? Any of us would be a fool
to think our literary perceptions superior to such critics as Sidney
or Dryden, and it is quite clear that Milton knew more that is
essential about the epic than anyone since. But it is also true that
no one in the seventeenth century could have written any of the
essays that follow or others like them that we think as natural as
daylight.

It must also be said that study of seventeenth-century English literature has certain advantages over earlier periods and certain disadvantages compared with later periods. The literature is almost entirely that from printed texts, with few of the problems of classical or medieval manuscripts at some hopelessly unrecoverable distance from their originals. The history of the century survives in reasonably full documentation and, in its first sixty years, certainly has been thoroughly gone over by contemporary historians. On the other hand, the literature of the century provides the last example of silence and darkness. The dates when most of Donne's poems were written can only be guessed, and no one knows when Milton wrote *Samson Agonistes*. Many poems can only be guessed to be by Suckling or Cleveland. Marvell's canon of Restoration satires is open to question, and their coarseness baffles anyone who has read his lyrics. We can call on little more than intuition to tell us of the forces that made so many young wits turn into grave divines or that made most of the major seventeenth-century writers change their religion at least once. None of us has ever endured the painful course of study inflicted on boys in late Renaissance schools and universities. None of us is confused over the motions of the sun and earth, or thinks constantly in terms of hierarchies, or invariably considers religion when political matters are discussed. We do stand at formidable distance from the writers of the seventeenth century, and we do require various means to interpret its literature. The essays that follow are exemplary, I believe, of current methods of interpreting that literature. The authors of the essays are leading American scholars and critics, their methods represent distinctive kinds of study, and their topics range from plays put on at Oxford as the century was beginning to lyrics written during the upheavals of midcentury.

The six essays in this book seem to me to fall naturally under three heads: Canon and Context, Controlling Ideas, and Interpretation. Along with textual criticism, study of canon and context involves kinds of study that most of us presume on trust when we pick up a book. So strong is the trust that the value of such study is sometimes doubted. It is not many years since an English don could assert in the letter pages of the *Times Literary Supplement* that the question of the authorship of *Macbeth* is an indifferent matter. (Of course he signed *his* name.) In considering the validity of such claims it is always useful to visit those two disciplines from which the study of vernacular literatures historically evolved: biblical and classical study. As is well known, the book of Daniel was of great interest to the eschatologically minded in the second third of the seventeenth century; even Isaac Newton felt compelled to write a commentary on it. Biblical scholars have shown in recent years that the oracles once ascribed to Daniel were not written during a Babylonian exile under Darius, who reigned over Persia in 521–486 B.C., but by an anonymous scribe using the figure of the good but dimly known Daniel to rouse his fellow Jews against the efforts of Antiochus Epiphanes to force the Jews into pagan idolatry in the three years following December, 167 B.C. The whole meaning of Daniel is not lessened, but it is very different, once we understand that in the second century B.C. Jews were told that the law of Moses was annulled, that on pain of death they must cease circumcision and observance of the sabbath, and that they must sacrifice what were to them unclean beasts to idols. The new attribution of Daniel to an unknown scribe and the dating of its oracles in the context of the heroic age of the Maccabees make a revolutionary difference to our understanding of a prophet, a difference of interpretation derived from facts of canon and context. To be sure, our understanding of no seventeenth-century work is likely to be so radically altered. But if some croquet box produces Donne's manuscripts in holograph and with dates, if Milton's commonplace book comes to light with dated drafts of his three major poems, or if a diary kept by Marvell is uncovered, seventeenth-century literary scholarship and criticism will never be quite the same. We do not expect these events ever to occur, but in our own day the studies by Rudolf Bultmann of the fourth Gospel and by Gerald F. Else of Aristotle's *Poetics* show how radically new interpretations may arise, even for writings whose "meanings" were thought wholly understood for centuries. If matters of canon and context be deemed propaedeutic, as in some sense no doubt they are, then we had best be sure that we have them right before we assume the grounds of our speculation. Airy castles rise not only in Spain.

Frank Livingstone Huntley's essay on the Parnassus plays, and especially the first part of *The Return from Parnassus*, seeks both an author to whose canon one or more of these plays may be assigned and the evidence that will justify such assignment. A number of people have been suggested as possible authors, and as Frank Huntley shows, we simply do not have sufficient evidence in hand to know certainly who the author was. And in a fine penultimate sentence, he sums up the wisdom of mature scholarship: "If there were documentary proof, of course, there would be no need of a hypothesis." What is the nature of such a hypothesis? Again, Frank Huntley tells us in a paragraph whose principles should be learned by every scholar. "Inevitably where external proof of authorship [as of much else] is lacking, the literary scholar must argue by probability. He makes a hypothesis to stand or fall not by a chain of reasoning (which breaks at its weakest link), but rather by explaining more historical facts and literary traits than any other. The hypothesis, furthermore, is made attractive by its solving other problems that hang upon the solution of this particular one." His case for the authorship of Joseph Hall seeks to put the principles in practice. His essay gives us, then, not merely methodological principles, important as those are, but also a practice showing how the method may be applied to other writers and other genres.

The major contextual discovery of our lifetime about the poetry of George Herbert has been that it supplies its own context, that the poems of *The Temple* are so ordered as to be read as a consecutive series. James Thorpe not only supplies a new context but also comments with wit and charity on the lack of knowledge of context possessed by most readers. As he well says, we commonly form acquaintance with a poet on the basis of a few selections:

Our ideas become fixed, and most of us are content that our last knowledge of them is also a limited fraction of their total production. So it may properly be for connoisseurs of poetry, and may their tribe increase. The world is full of poems, more good poems than anyone can ever read. As lovers of poetry, we probably do well to accept traditional selections and pass on to something else also good.

He goes on to remark on what is missing of Donne in the most widely read anthology, Dame Helen Gardner's *Metaphysical Poets*: more than half the *Songs and Sonnets*, both of the *Anniversaries*, and so on. James Thorpe is willing to hope that the student who misses the rest of Donne will gain some of Spenser, Wordsworth, and Yeats.

His point is that anything beyond that most attractive of enterprises, reading for the experience of reading alone—that is, anything we call criticism or scholarship—must take more into consideration. The critic or scholar of Donne "cannot afford such losses" as half of the *Songs and Sonnets*, "though I readily admit that some scholarly books create the impression that their authors stopped reading poetry at a tender age." He follows this sally with two propositions that make his essay, like Frank Huntley's, confessedly exemplary. His first proposition is the general one that "literary scholarship consists in finding rewarding contexts for poems," and of course he would include plays and novels under "poems." His second proposition offers a specific version of the first: that one context for Herbert's poetry is his prose, and in particular the *Outlandish Proverbs*. He has no difficulty in showing that the collection of aphoristic lore and the poems in *The Temple* share specific proverbs, or that a poem like "Charms and Knots" is entirely devoted to proverbs. He goes farther, showing by way of conclusion that the context he examines reveals "how essentially [Herbert] was concerned with ordinary human behavior, how he longed to have marks and aims that would be useful for himself and others, how his mind ran toward understandable imagery that could aid understanding." When we refer such a statement derived from contextual evidence to the poems in *The Temple*, we see how right James Thorpe is. And because the same qualities are to be found in *Outlandish Proverbs*, we find that the poems also illuminate the proverbs. Text and context may shift in this instance as examples of a single writer's coherent thought, and this central proposition is clearly the basic thesis of James Thorpe's essay.

No doubt literary interpretation involves attention to several kinds of controlling ideas. Two of the most fruitful are represented by the essays given us by Barbara K. Lewalski and Robert M. Adams. Barbara Lewalski shows how poems by three poets can be better understood in terms of variations on a single way of thought. Robert Adams uses a single dim figure in a lengthy epic to worry us into a new understanding of major features of the poem. For the one critic, the controlling idea is found by examining the ways in which poets thought in the seventeenth century. For the other, the idea is found in a poem of rival ideas and ideologies. Both critics show that the student of literature will advance understanding in major ways if a truly revealing idea can be found, whether in widespread ways of thinking or in an encounter with a specific poem.

Barbara Lewalski begins her examination of Herbert's poems where the state of the critical art had left them. She takes particular pains to argue that religious thought and, in particular, the typological belief that the New Testament fulfills the Old operate in *The Temple*. In a discussion that is a model of compression, she works both toward the more precise and the more general. She shows beyond doubt that we must think of specifically Protestant figuralism and its emphases if we are to understand the role played by typology in the poems by Herbert and other Protestant poets. Further, she makes clear how important the Psalms as interpreted by Protestants were to such figuralism, and even how important was the interpretation of part of a single psalm, the fifty-first. At this point the discussion widens to show how Herbert's figuralism works differently in the three parts of *The Temple*.

The understanding of Herbert is used as a means of getting to what is important in the religious thought of Vaughan's poetry, and she shows us how Vaughan takes certain Protestant emphases yet farther, sometimes to the extent of blurring a few orthodox features of figuralism. In particular, Vaughan gives us a consistent use of the Old Testament to provide types for his own experience, making himself, rather than the chief Person in the New Testament, the antitype. What defines the nature of such figuralism is, we are shown, the particular types chosen and their combination with such religious concerns as eschatology. Barbara Lewalski then moves from consideration of the figural systems of religious poetry to the religious system of a poem hitherto thought almost entirely secular, Marvell's *Upon Appleton House*. Marvell "intensifies" that Protestant emphasis shown in Herbert and Vaughan "and more remarkably, transfers that mode from the realm of devotional poetry to that of secular history." Because Puritans and sectaries had been doing just that for ten years or more in the active life of politics, there are no a priori grounds for thinking Marvell could not do so in a more contemplative retired life. The gist of Barbara Lewalski's interpretation lies in the following sentence: "In essence, Marvell assimilates the history of the Fairfax family and the topographical features of the Fairfax estate, as well as the experiences of the speaker who is making a progress around the estate, to the course of Providential history, by showing both speaker and family recapitulating certain biblical situations." The detailed argument provides the subtlest argument of a subtle essay (and a very subtle poem). For the more modest purposes of this introduction, however, the exemplary features of Barbara Lewalski's essay claim attention. Beginning with what is known (to one acquainted with the latest studies of her poets), she refines our understanding of the nature of Protestant figuralism and shows how Herbert in particular used it. Having delineated the kind of thought informing the poetry of a strong-minded and clear-headed Calvinist Anglican, she is able to turn to the looser thinking of Vaughan and make it clearer than it had seemed before. From such clarity and such looseness within Protestant private and devotional poetry she boldly takes us to an elusive poem at once contemplative and public. To repeat her closing words, "Significantly, for all three works [by Herbert, Vaughan, and Marvell] the typological mode provides in very different ways a unifying symbolic perspective which orders without at all reducing their rich multiplicity and complexity."

Such rich complexity translated into the student's difficulty forms the basis of the soliloquy or prologue with which Robert M. Adams begins his formal, even respectful, consideration of that curious Miltonic figure, Chaos, "the Anarch old / With falt'ring speech and visage incompos'd." Robert Adams suggests in that prologue that although the idea of chaos is ancient, very little has been written about it, and that as far as can be determined Milton's usage is unusual. (At least Henry More is the only one I know of who anticipates Milton.) How different, then, such a literary problem is from that explored by Barbara Lewalski, where the known mode of thought is refined and further used in its refined state to illuminate three poets. All of us seek to ask a few new questions about major works, and when we do, we feel that mingled exhilaration and giddiness that Robert Adams so well communicates. With a perceptible wrinkle in his brow and a wry smile, he recalls Hermann Hesse's *Blick ins Chaos*.

The essay addresses itself to the passage in the second book of *Paradise Lost* narrating the encounter of Satan and Chaos. Some interesting things begin to emerge. We must consider Satan as much as Chaos in this encounter, which leads us also to discover that as a concept chaos will be found important to the whole poem and to be mentioned as a word in all books but IV and IX. Robert Adams proceeds to muse on the relations between God (and Heaven), Chaos (and chaos), and Satan (and Hell). He comes to the conclusion that their dependence on one another is a matter of great convenience in Milton's poem, or at least to Milton. Certainly we need to understand the significance to Milton, and to the Christian thought he adapts, of his creating as persons and places what are essentially states and ideas. In a palinode that once again transforms into an argument on behalf of Chaos, Robert Adams handsomely treats the grave difficulties of trying to answer a new question about a major work. His style of thought and writing is so characteristic, so peculiar to himself, that the student emulating that alone would fail to see what makes this essay the exemplary piece it is. Robert Adams shows us that new questions, ipso facto, have less assured answers than old ones. For so new and difficult a problem in study of a poem, the important thing is the patient self-awareness with which he goes once again through an epic he has read so many times, in order that the validity of, and the answer to, a new question may be established. Whereas Barbara Lewalski must, as it were, re-form and refine catholic Christianity, Robert Adams must puzzle out the -doxy implied by something so fully hetero- as to have no seeming inner consistency at all. Both handle important ideas with facility, and both take the stances toward their ideas which the ideas appear to require.

The third pair of essays is presented under the head of "Interpretation." Of course in some sense all we can do is interpret, just as in some sense all we can think about are thoughts. But we recognize certain kinds of literary discussion as less interested in ideas or in the author or in much else that is important, but nonetheless very interested in accounting for the experience provided by such-and-such a text. The text under consideration by both critics is *Comus*, which is in a number of ways Milton's most difficult work. Both Louis L. Martz and Stanley E. Fish conclude that *Comus* is harmonious. Louis Martz does so by beginning with the literal harmonies of its music and proceeding thence to certain figurative implications. Stanley Fish takes the large and evident discords of the masque, and of criticism about it, to show how they may be resolved into concord.

Louis Martz clearly sets forth his plan of approach: from the literal music of *Comus* possessed by us to the music that we have probably lost; and from them he proceeds to musical allusions and descriptions in the poetry, and finally to that larger harmony of poetry. Such a line of interpretation puts into serious question our habitual consent to the words on the page. What we speak of as "Comus" from the edition we carry with us or take from the shelf is literally quite something other than what Louis Martz is talking about. His "Comus" not only has the Lawes music but has passages in our "Comus" removed to different contexts or divided among different speakers. We discover in reading this essay that our usual "Comus" has far less resemblance to Milton's masque than we had thought. We have a differently ordered and differently divided experience, and our experience is deficient in lacking music as well as in dramatic presentation.

Louis Martz seeks to supply us with as much as can be supplied or suggested of all that which we either do not have in our "Comus" or have differently. As with all kinds of literary study, including interpretation, his procedure entails discrimination. His Bibliographical Note alone clarifies and reorders our presumptions about the masque. His critical discussion at once acts as surrogate and reminder, by standing in the stead of what we have lost and by sadly reminding us that we have lost it. Nothing is newer than what has been lost, because we shall never be able to claim full possession of it. Perhaps to reassure us that Milton's masque leaves us with something perennially reliable for critical discussion, Louis Martz has his round in explaining what is meant by that Haemony which releases the Lady from her bonds. There is something endearing about the Miltonic cruces, and the solution offered in this essay well fits with its general subject. The last paragraphs of this discussion return us to the central experience of the masque set to music. In that music, and in its attention to time, the sage and serious doctrine of virginity finds its best context, a context transforming chastity into faith, hope, and charity.

Stanley E. Fish is far from regarding literary matters as settled, or from thinking all questions answered. The premise of his interpretation of *Comus* is in fact that "the verse forces the question," that the masque sets problems as part of the experience Milton wishes to create for us. "Fain would I something say, yet to what end?" So the Lady to Comus, who has neither ear nor soul to comprehend her moral principles. In the end, the Lady triumphs, but her conception of the place of herself and her principles in the world proves to be far more problematical than is revealed by most discussions of the masque. In similar fashion— and it is particularly satisfying to have interpretive method respond so congruently to the experience it discusses—Stanley Fish takes account of the many problems and questions discovered in *Comus* by what he somewhat grandly calls the " 'ingenious' party" of critics: in order "that we will become capable of reading the masque just as the conservative critics tell us it should be read." He would have us honor the difficulties and the problems posed in the reading of *Comus*, and he would have us understand

that such honoring entails a literary experience to which we de-
vote our best efforts as well as a respect for a morality as much
in jeopardy in our experience as it is for the Lady.

Louis L. Martz presents us with the problem that our version
of *Comus* is deficient and different. Stanley E. Fish presents us
with all manner of problems. To the one interpreter, what has
been lost must be recovered as far as possible by interpretation.
To the other, what may be lost and what is constantly at hazard
in the experience of reading are precisely our field of gain. Because both interpretations take negatives as their points of departure, and because both insist all along on difficulty, question,
and loss, it is truly remarkable that the result is much increased
respect for Milton, for *Comus*, and for our human powers to
understand. I do not believe it possible justly to accuse Stanley
Fish of failure to sympathize with the " 'ingenious' party" of
critical interpreters, or to put him into the camp of unthinking
literary conservatives, if indeed there be such a camp. But I do
believe that an interpretation accounting for as much of the dis-
sident and subtle as seems possible, while yet honoring the *con-
sensus lectorum*, surely stimulates consent. Louis Martz has in a
sense an easier time of it. His problems are specifiable partly because they are finally incapable of solution: we shall never be
able to attend a performance of *Comus* held before the Bridgewater family. The Lady and her brothers, after all, are engaged
in one of the basic human enterprises, getting home. Louis Martz
makes it beautifully clear that what we have lost is crucial, and
like the Attendant Spirit he has himself a music and a magic that
seems to let him throw a cloak of invisibility over the loss while
his music charms us.

Stanley Fish has no such easy time of it. He knows that he has
got to get home, and he agrees with the conservative critics what
and where home is. But he also knows, and certainly shows us,
that the problems of getting home are precisely what we most
honor and enjoy in *Comus*. He is not one of those critics whose
talk about a poem constantly assumes that one is reading only
about criticism of the poem.

I think that one other but related feature of his method of interpretation calls for some comment. His emphasis on what has
been termed "reader response" concerns not just his own response, which must finally be *his* Oedipus, as Sir Thomas
Browne put it, but also the responses represented by the comments of numerous critics. The appearance of the *Variorum*

Commentary on Milton's poems is just the moment to remind ourselves of the dangers in relying excessively on previous criticism and not enough on our reading itself of the masque. Stanley Fish demonstrates that the corpus of "secondary" study can provide assistance to our understanding of the "primary" thing, *Comus*, while not being a substitute for the main thing. Anyone engaged in teaching or writing about literature can find warm comfort in that assurance.

The fact that these essays are by others frees me to express my genuine liking for the variety and quality of literary enterprise shown in them. Like Robert Burton, I might well grant that an Introduction is a tedious thing, that if I saw the names and titles in the Contents, I would not myself think I needed any enthusiast to beckon me on, no golden bough or frenzied Sybil to tell me my way. On the other hand (which is very much Burton's favorite hand), why not communicate one's liking and respect for well-conducted literary discussion? Besides, as I suggested, these essays are exemplary as to method, useful even beyond the authors considered and beyond the century in which they lived. As such, my trust is that they will prove valuable to students as well as to established critics, that they will "delight" as Hobbes puts it, "all sorts of men, either by instructing the ignorant, or soothing the learned in their knowledge." But that distinction presents another problem, and I shall not attempt to solve it here.

CANON AND CONTEXT

I

JOSEPH HALL, JOHN MARSTON, AND

THE RETURNE FROM PARNASSUS

Frank Livingstone Huntley

As part of their Christmas festivities in the years 1598, 1599, and 1602, the boys of St. John's College at Cambridge, presumably aided by any other collegians they could draft, acted out three "Parnassus plays," which have become by their topical interest and dramatic excellence part of English literature.[1]

The first play, *The Pilgrimage to Parnassus*, describes two students on their way to the B.A. degree: the theologically inclined Studioso and the classicist-poet Philomusus. Passing through the "countries" of Logic, Rhetoric, and Philosophy, they successfully withstand their tempters: the ministerial Studioso rejects a Ramistic Puritan, and Philomusus the poet turns his back on a drunken Aretine. Both of them, however, are attracted to Amoretto, reading Ovid, despite Ingenioso's warning that Hobson makes more money renting twelve nags than they could writing two hundred books.

The next two plays together are called *The Returne from Parnassus*. In the first of these, having attained their degrees, the boys are set adrift in the real world, where, soon discovering that nobody seems willing either to buy their poetry or pay them

[1] I am grateful to the Trustees of The Folger Shakespeare Library for granting me an eight-week Fellowship in the spring of 1970 for a project loosely entitled "To begin a book on Bishop Joseph Hall." For their critical reading of this "chapter," I thank my colleagues Edmund Creeth, Ejner Jensen, and John Knott.

living wages as schoolmaster or chaplain, they threaten to accept the bribe for "perverting" to Rome. The second part of *The Returne*, subtitled "The Scourge of Simony," opens with the boys reading the newly published *Belvedere or the Muses' Garden* and lampooning every contemporary poet in it except "Mr. Shakespeare," whose *Venus and Adonis* they think very good. As many as seventeen new characters are added (not counting "fiddlers"), each one remarkably differentiated. The comic turns of plot are more complex, and the dialogue wittier. While waiting for a benefice, which is sold to an ignoramus for a hundred pounds, the boys try to live by pretending to be a French physician and his man, then as actors with two bedraggled characters named Burbage and Kempe, and finally as wandering fiddlers. After firing a few initial shots in "the war of the theatres" and complaining of this unappreciative world, they retire to the Arcadian simplicity of a shepherd's life in Kent.

This, the second part of *The Returne from Parnassus*, was the only one of the three that was printed (twice in 1606). It stood alone until the Rev. W. D. Macray, Bodley's librarian, discovered in Thomas Hearne's collection the manuscripts of *The Pilgrimage to Parnassus* and the first part of *The Returne from Parnassus*. In 1866 he published the first edition of the comic trilogy.[2]

Immediately speculation on their authorship began, based on the charade-like hints in the prologues of the last two plays.[3] Of the author of *The Pilgrimage* the prologue to the first *Returne* says:

> Surelie it made our poet a staide man,
> Kepte his proude necke from baser lambskins weare,
> Had like to have made him senior sophister,
> He was faine to take his course by Germanie
> Ere he coulde gett a silie poore degree.
> Hee neuer since durst name a peece of cheese,
> Thoughe Chessire seems to priuiledge his name.[4]

---

[2] *The Pilgrimage to Parnassus with the Two Parts of the Returne from Parnassus: Three Comedies performed in St. John's College Cambridge A.D. MDXCVII–MDCI* (Oxford, 1886).

[3] J. B. Leishman, ed., *The Three Parnassus Plays, 1598–1601* (London, 1949), Introduction, pp. 26–34; and Marjorie L. Reyburn, "New Facts and Theories about the Parnassus Plays," *Publications of The Modern Language Association of America*, LXXIV (1959), 325–335.

[4] Leishman, *Three Parnassus Plays*, p. 135. All quotations from the plays are from this edition; the references hereafter are incorporated in my text.

So it has been argued that William Dodd, the only Cheshire name at St. John's College at the time, was the author. Again, John Day, who spelled his name "Dey," which means dairyman or a maker of cheese, has been named as the author. Again, it has been proposed that by "Germany" is meant "Holland"; therefore William Holland wrote the first play. On grounds like these one might build a better argument for John Weever of Queen's. He was well known as a witty poet to both Hall and Marston; he greatly admired Shakespeare's erotic verse; and his famous epigram on Gullio is actually used in the first *Returne from Parnassus* (l. 959, p. 182). He may well have given his friends fears that he would never graduate because of his drinking (Germany was notorious for its lack of sobriety). And since the Weaver is the principal river in the county of Cheshire, "Cheshire seems to privilege his name"—John Weever.

Slightly less obscure hints, this time of a possibly new authorship, appear in the prose and poetic prologues of the second part of *The Returne from Parnassus*.[5] This "is the last time that is, the Authors wit wil turne vpon the toe in this vaine" (p. 222) is what the manuscript version says, but the 1606 printed version has: "that is both the first & the last time," which would make the author of the last play a different man from the author of the *Pilgrimage* and from the author of the first *Returne*. The poetic prologue to the last play tells us:

> In Scholers fortunes twise forlorne and dead
> Twise hath our weary pen earst laboured,
> Making them Pilgrims to *Pernassus* hill,
> Then penning their returne with ruder quill.
> Now we present vnto each pittying eye
> The schollers progresse in their miserye.
>
> [P. 224]

In his summary of the problem of authorship, Leishman (p. 31) concludes that there are two authors: one for the *Pilgrimage* and the other for the two *Returnes*. He assumes that "ruder," in the rhetoric of frontal matter, means "less competent" in a purposefully humble sense, hence a different author. But he also gives evidence (p. 27) that at one time the three plays were known as "Pilgrimage," "Returne," and "Progresse"; indeed the prologue just quoted does break the trilogy between the first two plays

---

[5] For documentation of chronology see *ibid.*, p. 26.

and the third, "ruder" intending merely "harsher" or more satirical. The last play shows artistic superiority in plot, character,
and wit; and a marked increase in satirical acerbity. The problem
is: who wrote it?

Inevitably where external proof of authorship is lacking, the
literary scholar must argue by probability. He makes a hypothesis to stand or fall not by a chain of reasoning (which breaks at
its weakest link), but rather by explaining more historical facts
and literary traits than any other. The hypothesis, furthermore,
is made attractive by its solving other problems that hang upon
the solution of this particular one.

I shall argue, then, that Joseph Hall (1574–1656), Fellow
of Emmanuel College, well-known man of letters and future
churchman, may have had a hand in all three plays and was the
major author of the second *Returne from Parnassus*. And I shall
arrange the evidence to support my case in three major propositions ranging from fact to reasonable inference, as follows: (1)
that certain facts, such as the verbal parallels in the Parnassan
plays to Hall's published work and the absence in Hall's satires
of direct attack on Marston, coupled with Marston's hatred of
Hall, demand an explanation; (2) that in view of the satire on
Marston in the second *Returne from Parnassus*, the origin of
Marston's hitherto unexplained attack on Hall may be his con-
viction that Hall was mainly responsible for it; and (3) that
Joseph Hall might very well have had reasons for concealing his
authorship, as his chosen career would have been jeopardized had
he claimed all the literary effusions of his youth. It will become
apparent that John Marston is the crux of my argument.

I

Obviously indisputable is that the Parnassan plays are filled
with verbal parallels to Hall's *Vergidemiae*. Macray, the first
editor of all three plays, wrote: "A comparison with Bishop
Hall's *Satires* brings to view a great similarity alike in subjects
and in language. The second book of *Satires* deals, in fact, with
many of the abuses of which our unknown author treats" [6]—
namely, poverty-stricken scholars, charlatan lawyers, quack doc-
tors, simony, hiring a well-educated tutor at starvation wages.
Many of the personae are similar too; for example, Ingenioso's

[6] "Preface," p. x.

description of Amoretto is almost exactly like Hall's description of Gallio. The Parnassan Gullio and Hall's Gallio are both son-neteers; and most of the Parnassan wits admire Spenser, as does Joseph Hall.[7]

Not a single passage in the plays reflects sarcastically upon the writing of Joseph Hall. Though I have selected the following verbal parallels from dozens at random, all seven of them link Hall's *Vergidemiae* to the second part of *The Returne from Parnassus*, the only one of the three plays, as if to reflect superior authorship, that was printed:

1. a) Hall, I, i, 8–9, p. 12.[8]
        Nor can I bide to pen some hungry *Scene*
        For *thick-skin eares*, and vndiscerning eyne.
    b) *Parnassus*, 2d *Returne*, IV, 1340–1341, p. 305.
        The [servile] current of my slyding verse
        Gently shal runne into his *thick-skind eares*.

2. a) Hall, I, ii, 25–26, p. 13.
        And where they wont sip of the simple floud,
        Now tosse they *bowles of Bacchus boyling blood*.
    b) *Parnassus*, 2d *Returne*, I, vi, 503, p. 257.
        There quaffing *bowles of Bacchus blood* ful nimbly.

3. a) Hall, II, ii, 15–16, p. 24.
        Scorne ye the world before it do complaine,
        And *scorne the world that scorneth you againe*.
    b) *Parnassus*, 2d *Returne*, I, iv, 399, p. 251.
        Ile *scorne the world that scorneth me againe*.

4. a) Hall, II, iii, 23–24, p. 26.
        Each home-bred science percheth in the *chaire*,
        Whiles sacred arts *grouell on the ground*sell bare.
    b) *Parnassus*, 2d *Returne*, II, i, 557–559, pp. 261–262.
        Oh how it greeues my vexed soule to see
        Each painted asse in *chayre* of dignitye;
        And yet we *grouell on the ground* alone.

5. a) Hall, II, iv, 11–12, p. 27, on the medical fashion of uroscopy.
        And spie out maruels in each Vrinall,
        And *tumble vp the filths that from them fall*.
    b) *Parnassus*, 2d *Returne*, I, ii, 143–146, p. 228.
        . . . like a needy Phisitian to stand whole yeares
        tooting *and tumbling the filth that falleth*.

---

[7] Leishman, Introduction, p. 54.

[8] All my quotations from Hall's *Vergidemiae* are from A. Davenport's edition, *The Collected Poems of Joseph Hall* (Liverpool, 1949). The references occur within my text. Here I have omitted textual italics in order to underscore verbal similarities.

6. a) Hall, IV, i, 72, p. 51.
    His Eares hang lauing like ø *new-lug'd swine.*
  b) *Parnassus*, 2d *Returne*, V, iv. 2195, p. 365.
    Like a great *swine*, by his *long laue-eard lugges.*
7. a) Hall, V, iv, 14, p. 86.
    To drag his *Tumbrell* through the *staring Cheape.*
  b) *Parnassus*, 2d *Returne*, I, i, 110–113, p. 226.
    Nor can it mongst our gallants prayses reape,
    Unlesse it be [y]done in *staring Cheape*,
    In a sinne-guilty *Coach.*

Indeed, the parallels between these witty but still anonymous plays, especially the second *Returne*, and Hall's published satires are so numerous and so telling as to have brought the late editor of Hall's *Collected Poems*, Professor A. Davenport of Liverpool, to the very verge of my thesis: "I would not positively affirm that Hall had a share in the writing of the Parnassus Plays, but it is demonstrable that the writer, whoever he was, knew *Vergidemiae* with suspicious intimacy and shared Hall's critical views." [9]

Equally indisputable is that Marston launched a bitter attack on Hall in his *Certayne Satires*, published with *The Metamorphosis of Pygmalion's Image*. These attacks Marston continued in *The Scourge of Villanie* of 1598, reissued twice in 1599. To explain Marston's hatred of Hall, Grosart and Bullen conjectured that Hall had seen a manuscript version of *Pygmalion's Image* before he wrote his three books of *Byting Satyres* (1598).[10]

But more recent scholarship does not find the cause in Hall's known published work. Ford E. Curtis, in his 1932 Cornell dissertation, concluded that "there is in Hall no unmistakeable reference to Marston." [11] And though Davenport links the attack to the earlier Harvey-Nashe controversy, even he comes to this negative conclusion: "Of the quarrel between Marston and Hall no completely satisfactory account can be given." [12] Anthony Caputi, in *John Marston, Satirist*, thinks that the only item that

---

[9] Introduction, p. xviii, n. 1.
[10] A. B. Grosart, ed., *The Complete Poems of Joseph Hall* (Manchester, 1875), Introduction, pp. xxii–xxvi; A. H. Bullen, ed., *The Works of John Marston*, 3 vols. (Boston, 1887), I, ixx, xx.
[11] As quoted by Anthony Caputi, *John Marston, Satirist* (Ithaca, N.Y., 1961), p. 35.
[12] *The Collected Poems of Joseph Hall*, p. xxviii.

might have been the ground for the attack is the epigram on "Kinsayder," Marston's chosen pseudonym, supposedly pasted by Hall into copies of Marston's book as they lay in the stalls at Cambridge. But the evidence that this is Hall's comes from John Marston; and Arnold Stein, R. M. Alden, K. Schultz, and Morse Allen all feel that the epigram is not by Hall.[13] Acknowledging its poetic inferiority, Davenport nevertheless includes it in Hall's canon (p. 101) as possibly Hall's "reactio" to Marston. If so, it is an effect and not a cause. How personally Marston took some of Hall's general criticism of contemporary poetry in *Vergidemiae* we do not know. The fact is that Hall's published satires do not directly name Marston or his poetry or even throw a particularizing glance in Marston's direction.

On the other hand, the Parnassan plays, especially the second *Returne*, are filled with libelous slurs on John Marston. The character Furor Poeticus in the final play, actually referred to as "Kinsayder," is a merciless lampoon. When Ingenioso reads the name "John Marston" from Bodenham's *Belvedere*, Judicio cries: "What *Monsier Kinsayder*, lifting vp your legge and pissing against the world? Put vp man, put vp for shame" (2d *Returne*, I, ii, 267–268, p. 241). The name "Kinsayder" is connected to "kinsing," the act of docking dogs' tails, and the parody bristles with Marstonian dog-images. A perusal of Leishman's parallels and allusions to Marston's poems (pp. 82–92) and of the index (under "Parnassus") to Davenport's edition of Marston's poems makes argument unnecessary, but a few quotations from the two texts will show how vicious their tone is.

1. a) Marston, *Certaine Satyres*, V, 49–50, p. 88.
      In strength of lust and *Venus* surquedry
      Rob'd fifty wenches of virginity.[14]
   b) *Parnassus, Pilgrimage*, IV, 479–490, p. 120.
      Theile freelie giue what ere youre luste shall craue
      And make you melte in Venus surque[d]rie.
2. a) Marston, *Scourge*, VIII, 143–144, p. 154.
      I am not saplesse, old, or rumatick,
      No *Hipponax* mishapen stigmatick. . . .
   b) *Parnassus, Pilgrimage*, II, 210, 215, pp. 105–106. The

---

13 See *ibid.*, p. 263; and Caputi, pp. 34–35.
14 All my quotations of Marston are from A. Davenport, ed., *The Poems of John Marston* (Liverpool, 1961), the references again incorporated in my text. It is fortunate that a single editor of Davenport's ability should have edited these two satirists.

phrase "old Stigmaticke" occurs in a speech that also
mentions "Kinsaders Satyrs."

3. a) Marston, *Scourge*, "To Detraction," ll. 7–12, p. 95.
Know that the *Genius*, which attendeth on,
And guides my powers intellectuall,
Holds in all vile repute *Detraction*,
My soule an essence metaphisicall,
  That in the basest sort scornes *Critickes* rage,
  Because he knowes his sacred parentage.

  b) *Parnassus*, 2d *Returne*, III, iv, 1301–1304, p. 303.
Furor Poeticus: "By that caelestiall fier within my brayne
That giues a liuing genius to my lines:
How ere my dulled intellectuall
Capres lesse nimbly than it did a fore.

4. a) Marston, *Certaine Satyres*, V, 169, p. 92.
The subject is too sharp for my dull quill.

  b) *Parnassus*, 2d *Returne*, I, vi, 471, p. 256.
Furor Poeticus: "Who's that runs headlong on my quills
sharpe poynt?"

One can only conclude, as others have, that whoever wrote the
Parnassus plays did not care much for the poetry of John Marston, and that especially in the second *Returne* he was not afraid
to draw Furor Poeticus as parodying Marston's satirical style.

So far there has been no room for argument. We have known
for a long time that a series of events culminated in a one-sided
quarrel; that Hall's *Vergidemiae* are liberally quoted in the Parnassan plays, that Hall does not particularize Marston in his *Vergidemiae*, and that Furor Poeticus in the second *Returne from
Parnassus* obviously satirizes Marston.

II

We must now move into a wider circle and ask questions
whose answers are bound to be more tentative. What caused
Marston's hatred of Hall? Mere jealousy? Both poets had joined
the new school of young satirists, but Hall had preceded Marston
in publication by a whole year. And yet no poet as proud as
Marston would attack a fellow poet so viciously on grounds of
jealousy alone lest he confess his own poems to be inferior. Could
the jibes against Marston in the Parnassan plays be the cause of
Marston's attack? Another way of asking the same question is

this: Why is it that Marston in his published work often combined his attacks on Hall with his quite justified resentment of the parody of his poetic style and person in *The Returne from Parnassus*?

That he does do this may be demonstrated by documenting passages of Marston's vilification of Joseph Hall that contain within themselves "reactio's" to the St. John's College Parnassan plays. Some examples follow.

In *The Scourge of Villanie* (XI, 104–106, p. 170), Marston uses against Hall the names of "honest Phylo" and "judiciall Musus," which combine by accident or design to form Philomusus, the main character in all three Parnassan plays.

In *The Scourge* (III, 11–18, pp. 114–115), Marston writes: "What Academick starued Satyrist / Would once a thrice-turn'd bone-pick'd subject gnaw / When swarmes of Mountebancks, & Bandeti. . . ." The "thrice-turn'd bone," another dog-metaphor, may allude to the Parnassan trilogy,[15] while the term "mountebanks" suggests actors on a stage.

In Satire IX the repeated word "apes" in the plural, as though Marston had more than merely Joseph Hall in mind, refers to poetic imitators, but it could also suggest the "apish imitation" of the mimic stage:

> Come downe yee Apes, or I will strip you quite,
> Baring your bald tayles to the peoples sight.
>
> [IX, 11–12, p. 158]

"Athens apes" (l. 21) means Cambridge, and Marston's phrase "furr'd with beard" and "cas'd in a Satin suite" (l. 15) may well glance at college boys costumed in a play.

In the same satire, Marston says of Hall:

> O senceless prose, iudiciall poesie,
> How ill you'r link'd. This affectation,
> To speake beyond mens apprehension
> How Apish tis. When all in fusten sute
> Is cloth'd a huge *nothing*, all for repute
> Of profound knowledge, when profoundnes knowes
> There's nought containd, but only seeming showes.
>
> [IX, 65–71, p. 160]

---

[15] Assuming that all three plays had been written by 1598, though the performance of the last play came later.

Although the main target of Satire IX is Joseph Hall, the fifth line of it, "O how on tiptoes proudly mounts my Muse" had been mocked in *Parnassus*: "Endite a tiptoe-strouting poesy" (2d *Returne*, I, v, 503, p. 258) and "my high tiptoe-strowting poesye" (*ibid.*, III, v, 1345, p. 305). The "fusten sute" of course refers to style, but with "showes" it may allude to a stage production. The "Athens ape" that "yaule[s] *auditores humanissimi*" merely makes fun of Hall's collegiate status by using a stock Latin phrase from a typical undergraduate prolusion, but the Latin phrase had been used as a nickname for an academic in *The Pilgrimage to Parnassus* (V, 633, p. 127). Most importantly, Hall's published satires are all poetry, and Marston's disparaging poetry and prose "ill-linked" in this strike against Joseph Hall can only refer to the Parnassus plays, which actually do combine prose and poetry.

In the eighth satire of the first book *Vergidemiarum*, Hall had written:

> Hence ye profane: mell not with holy things
> That *Sion* muse from *Palestina* brings.
> *Parnassus* is transform'd to *Sion* hill. . . .
> Yea and the Prophet of heauenly Lyre,
> Great *Salomon*, sings in the English Quire,
> And is become a newfound Sonetist,
> Singing his loue, the holy spouse of Christ:
> Like as she were some light-skirts of the rest
> In mightiest Ink-hornismes he can thither wrest.
>
> [I, viii, 1-12, p. 19]

This poem Marston is certainly answering in *Reactio*:

> Ye *Granta's* white Nymphs, come & with you bring
> Some sillabub, whilst he doth sweetly sing
> Gainst *Peters* teares, and *Maries* mouing moane,
> And like a fierce enraged Boare doth foame
> At sacred Sonnets, O daring hardiment!
> At *Bartas* Sweet Semaines, raile impudent
> At *Hopkins*, *Sternhold*, and the *Scottish* King.
>
> [ll. 35-41, p. 82]

Hall's and Marston's references seem to tally well as far as they concern Southwell's sacred poetry, Gervase Markham's *The Poem of Poems*, or *Sion's Muse*, and perhaps Lodge's *The Teares of Marie Mother of God*. But though Hall merely bids du Bartas

of France and Ariosto of Italy to yield to the English Spenser
(I, iv, 25–28), where does he "raile impudent" against du Bartas,
Hopkins, Sternhold, and the Scottish king? A passage from the
second *Returne from Parnassus* supplies the answer. When the
names of Henry Lok (Locke) and Thomas Hudson are read out
from *Belvedere*, Judicio says: "*Locke* and *Hudson*, sleep you
quiet shauers, among the shauings of the presse, and let your
bookes lie in some old nooke amongst old bootes and shooes, so
you may [happ to] auoyd my censure" (p. 241). Henry Lok in
1591 had contributed a sonnet to the *Essayes of a Prentice* by
James VI of Scotland. Lok's *Christian Passions* (1593) contained
a hundred sonnets, and his *Ecclesiasticus* (1597), "abridged and
also periphristically dilated in English Poesie," added 306 sonnets as well as "Sunday Psalms of David, translated into verse."
His partner in Parnassan crime, Thomas Hudson, had dedicated
his translation of du Bartas as *The History of Judith in forme of
a Poem* to His Majesty James VI of Scotland, and its frontal
matter contains a royal sonnet. The book was published in Edinburgh in 1584. Marston included Hopkins and Sternhold as in-
veterate Psalm-versifiers sure to be in Joseph Hall's hate list, but
there is no doubt that he got Hall "rail[ing] impudent" at "Bartas Sweet Semaines and at the Scottish King" not from *Vergidemiae*, I, viii, but from the second *Returne from Parnassus*.
The very next poet for Parnassan condemnation, after Lok and
Hudson, is John Marston as Monsieur Kinsayder lifting up his
leg "to piss against the world" (p. 241).

A similar proof comes in Marston's "Reactio" (*Certaine
Satyres*, IV, 81–82, p. 83), where Marston asks:

> What, shall not *Rosamond*, or *Gaueston*,
> Ope their sweet lips without detraction?

These are obvious references to Daniel's *The Complaint of Rosa-
mund* (1592) and Drayton's *The Legend of Piers Gaveston*
(1594). Marston is responding to Hall's *Vergidemiae*, I, v; but
Professor Davenport confesses (*Marston*, p. 245) that he can
see no clear trace in Hall's poem of criticism of these two pieces;
he had made the same confession in 1949 in his commentary on
Hall (pp. xlix and 168). Davenport's dilemma, however, is resolved by seeking background for Marston's "reactio" not in
Hall's *Vergidemiae* but in the second *Returne from Parnassus*.
There the college wits say:

> Sweete hony dropping *Daniell* may wage
> Warre with the proudest big Italian
> That melts his heart in sugred sonetting:
> Onely let him more sparingly make vse
> Of others wit, and vse his owne the more.
>
> [I, ii, 235–239, pp. 238–239]

Without break there follows immediately a censure of the author of *The Legend of Piers Gaveston*:

> *Draytons* sweete muse is like a sanguine dy,
> Able to rauish the rash gazers eye.
>
> [ll. 246–251]

Only, the boys continue, Drayton lacks one true mark of a poet of our times, that is, "hee cannot swagger it well in a Tauerne." Marston's attack on Hall's Satire I, v, of *Vergidemiae*, then, embraces a criticism expressed in *Parnassus* as if one man, Joseph Hall, were responsible for them both.

In *The Scourge*, XI (110 ff., p. 170), Marston writes of "judiciall Musus," who is Hall:

> . . . Wilt thou credite me
> He neuer writ one line in poesy,
> But once at Athens in a theame did frame
> A paradox in prayse of Vertues name.

I suggest that this refers to the poetic speech spoken by Consiliodorus near the beginning of *The Pilgrimage to Parnassus*. One of the longest speeches in the whole trilogy (seventy-six lines), it actually is a theme in praise of virtue. As the young pilgrims start on their journey, Consiliodorus, a Dametas-like figure, advises them to beware of flatterers, carousers, and lecherers; he counsels academic youth not to hope for this world's goods but instead to be diligent "to make the vallies heare with admiration / Those songs which youre refined tounge shall singe" (I, i, 101–102, p. 99). And yet, in view of the "frame" in which the speech occurs, that is the two plays of satire that follow it, to Marston it may very well be a paradox. It seems as though he refers to the same Parnassan speech in "Reactio," which is a vehement denunciation of Joseph Hall:

> . . . thus it is when pitty Priscians
> Will needs step up to be Censorians.

> When once they can in true skan's verses frame
> *A braue* Encomium *of good vertues name.*
> Why thus it is, when Mimick Apes will striue
> With Iron wedge the trunks of Oakes to riue.
>
> [*Certaine Satyres*, IV, 103–108, p. 84]

A peculiarity of this long speech in praise of virtue is that it is mainly in blank verse, a fact that may lie behind Marston's phrase "true skan's verses" as opposed to rimed.

Still smarting at the picture of himself in the St. John's College play, Marston seems to be convinced that the author is a Puritan, perhaps a member of Emmanuel College.[16] Marston (II, 56, p. 73) speaks of Hall as that "deuote meale-mouth'd Precisean." Similarly, the whole of "Satyra Nova," added to the second edition of his book and dedicated to Edward Guilpin, once of Emmanuel College, is an attack on Hall. In it Marston says:

> Cryes beard-graue *Dromus*, when alas, God knowes,
> His toothles gums nere chaw but outward showes.
> Poore Budgeface, bowcase sleeue, but let him passe,
> *Once fur and beard shall priuledge an Asse.*
>
> [ll. 23–26, pp. 163–164]

This is the poem in which Marston quotes the epigram on Kinsayder which he accuses Hall of having pasted in the copies of his book. The "toothles gums" are Hall's "Toothless Satyres," and though Dromio is a slave in Terence he is also a clown in *The Pilgrimage to Parnassus*. Again, the "fur and beard" bespeaks an actor; and as for "Budgeface," referring to an academic hood trimmed with white lamb's wool, Davenport comments: "If so, Dromus will be a Fellow, perhaps of Emmanuel" (p. 353).

Finally, in the ninth satire of *The Scourge*, entirely devoted to assailing Joseph Hall, Marston writes:

> Why lookes neate *Curus* all so simperingly?
> Why babbles thou of deepe Diuinitie?
> And of that sacred testimoniall?
> Liuing voluptuous like a *Bacchanall?*
> Good hath thy tongue: but thou ranke Puritan,
> I'll make an Ape as good a Christian.
> I'le force him chatter, turning vp his eye

---

[16] See Philip J. Finkelpearl, *John Marston of the Middle Temple* (Cambridge, Mass., 1969), p. 90.

> Looke sad, goe graue, Demure ciuilitie
> Shall seeme to say, *Good brother, sister deere.* . . .
>   Disguised *Messaline,*
> I'le teare thy maske, and bare thee to the eyne
> Of hissing boyes, if to the Theaters
> I finde thee once more come for lecherers
> To satiate.
>
> [ll. 105–125, pp. 161–162]

If the inspiration for this anger were the *Vergidemiae,* there would be no need to tear off a mask since Hall is speaking there in his own person. Rather, Marston places the sniveling Puritan, Joseph Hall, in a theater, evidently disguised in a costume, acting in a stage piece whose audience is made up of boys: "I'le teare thy maske, and bare thee to the eyne / Of hissing boyes, if to the Theaters / I finde thee once more come."

One may conclude that Marston's quarrel with Hall stems from Marston's belief that Hall was very much behind the satirical portrait in the character of Furor Poeticus, called Kinsayder, who appears in the second *Returne from Parnassus,* written and acted in St. John's College, Cambridge. Although the first performance of the second *Returne* took place in December, 1601, whereas Marston published his reaction in 1598 and 1599, we do not know how long before its first performance the play was actually written. Its prologue says: "What is presented here, is an old musty showe, that hath laine this twelfe-moneth in the bottome of a coale-house" (p. 220).

And what about the minor problem of Joseph Hall's so-called "lost Pastorals"? [17] In his most savage attack on Hall, Marston asks with obvious sarcasm, "Will not his Pastorals indure for euer?" ("Reactio," l. 148, p. 85). The term could not possibly apply to the satires *Vergidemiarum* in whose context it appears. In "The King's Prophecy" of 1603, Hall refers to an early work of his own, a translation of Vergil's fourth eclogue in which (so he says) he had hailed the birth of Henry the Prince, first son of James VI of Scotland (st. 17, p. 112). There is no other record of this piece, which may have been a college exercise, since Henry was born in 1593. In 1598 Marston could not have been

---

[17] The problem of Hall's "lost Pastorals" was first mentioned by J. P. Collier (*Bridgewater Catalogue* [London, 1887], p. 139); expanded by Thomas Corser (*Collectanea Anglo-Poetica,* VII [1887], p. 134); also by A. H. Bullen (*Works of John Marston,* III [1887], p. 286 n. 1); it is mentioned by Professor Davenport, *Hall's Poems,* Introduction, p. xvii.

referring to Hall's 1603 notation of it; and if he knew about it he would have used the singular, not the plural: "Will not his Pastoralls indure foruer?" The Parnassan plays, on the other hand, show great admiration for the pastorals of Spenser, and the main characters actually become shepherds. As when Marston asked Hall to "show vs the true forme of Dametas face" (*Certaine Satyres*, I, 120, p. 70), he seems to be wishing here that Hall had left the Parnassan plays all pastoral and not have added the satire. They *are* pastoral; at the end of the trilogy, Philomusus says:

> Perhaps some happy wit, with feeling hand,
> Hereafter may recorde the pastorall
> Of the two schollers of *Pernassus* hill,
> And then our scene may end and haue content.
>
> [P. 366]

Hall had ended his introductory poem to *Vergidemiae*, "Defiance to Envy," which Marston is savagely parodying in "Reactio," with an idyllic view of pastoral verse. "Speake ye attentive swaynes that heard me late," he says, and vows hereafter to write not pastoral but only satire: "At Colins feete I throw my yeelding reed." Are the Parnassan plays Hall's "pastorals" that the Cambridge swains had "lately heard," and is Marston wishing that his enemy had kept to the pastoral strain of innocent pilgrims to Parnassus? We shall never know for certain.

Meanwhile, however, the best way to account for Marston's associating his hatred of Joseph Hall with his resentment of the Cambridge players is to grant that in 1598 and 1599 Marston believed Joseph Hall to be the main author of the Parnassan plays.

III

Moving into an even wider circle, that of problems in Hall's biography, we may enquire, finally, why there can be no documentary proof that Joseph Hall wrote the second *Returne from Parnassus*. Of all the candidates for authorship Hall has the best reasons for concealment. After making a reputation at Cambridge for satirical writing, he decided, probably during the last year of Queen Elizabeth's life, to become a churchman within the Establishment. To have published two volumes of satires while still a student is enough for fame; to have published them when sedition

and treason were bringing laws down upon the heads of poets
made him notorious. The very entitling of his second three books
as "Byting Satyres" whereas the first three were "Toothles
Satyres" may bear some relationship to the fact that *The Returne
from Parnassus* differs from *The Pilgrimage to Parnassus* as the
harshness of the economic and literary world differs from the
joys and temptations of academic life. The "ruder quill" of the
prologue to the second play, therefore, instead of meaning "in-
competent" or "unskilled," may only signify satire as being
"harsh" and "rugged" in its verse. In the opening of his 1597 publication Hall himself had said: "The ruder Satyre should goe
rag'd and bare: / And show his rougher and his hairy hide" ("His
Defiance to Enuie," ll. 76–77, p. 9). Thus the satire, especially
in the last play, shifts from that of Horace to Juvenalian wrath
heaped upon simony and Philistinism, arch-sins of altar and pen.
As the curtain rises enter "Ingenioso, with Iuvenall in his hand,"
whom Judicio greets with, "What, Ingenioso, carrying a Vine-
gar bottle about thee?" The boys at St. John's College needed
a Joseph Hall of Emmanuel to complete the Christmas satires
they had begun.

But in the very month that the second performance of the second part of *The Returne from Parnassus* took place, Joseph Hall
received the benefice from the Drury family at Hawsted, Suffolk.
With the arrival of James I the following year, his decision was
set. He wrote a laudatory poem to welcome the new king, in
which he said to His Majesty:

> Pardon thou the while
> Mine high attempt, harsh verse, and ruder style.
>
> [St. 31, p. 115]

After that he became Prince Henry's favorite chaplain, one of
King James's constant preachers at Theobalds and elsewhere,
royal representative to theological synods in Scotland and at
Dort, and was to hold two successive bishoprics in the Anglican
church. A religious man, he must have become convinced that
his escaping punishment in 1599 from Archbishop Whitgift's
order was an act of Providence in his peculiar behalf. Marston's
and Hall's satires were both condemned to be publicly burned,
but Hall's were reprieved.

Not only had Joseph Hall decided upon a courtly and ecclesiastical career, but he felt called upon to become a serious writer;

hence he might well withdraw from a poetomachia he had stumbled into by writing an apparently nonserious university skit. As a Christian he wanted to do something closer to men's conscience, so he wrote one of the earliest English books of *Meditations* (1606). After taking the negative view common to scolding, he wanted to write something more positive; hence the first of its genre in England, his *Characters of Virtues and Vices* (1608). He felt the necessity, as Marston and others did, to separate the satirical condemnation of vices from that of the mere religious zealot by adopting a more moderate, humble, and honest stance; hence the volumes of his own *Epistle* in English (1608–1611), a genre to become popular as the century wore on. The moral position of the satirist is also that of the Stoic, above the pettiness of small minds; hence Hall's decision to become "the English Seneca." [18] These are some of the reasons why Hall should remain anonymous before and after he saw the second *Returne from Parnassus* twice acted in 1601 and 1602 and twice in print in 1606.

But Hall was in Emmanuel, and these are St. John's College plays. While a student at Cambridge, Hall is known to have been so popular for his wit and oratory as to have joined with friends from other colleges in their display. In 1597, for example, he took part in the festivities that welcomed the Earl of Essex to Cambridge. George Coke, writing a Latin letter to his brother John, who was staying with his friend Fulke Greville at Essex House in the Strand, describes the occasion. Among those taking part, Coke says, were Sutton of King's, Stanton of St. John's, Sharton of Trinity, and Braithwaite and Joseph Hall of Emmanuel. [19] This was the year Hall published his first volume of satires.

The Parnassan device of a *"voyage imaginaire,"* moreover, is shared by Joseph Hall's early "novel." Some time long before it was published in 1605, Hall composed in Latin the dystopia called *Mundus Alter et Idem* (the world different and yet the

[18] In a sense the role of a great satirist requires that he outgrow it. For this reason Hall is superior as a satirical poet to Marston (or for that matter to any other candidate for the authorship of the Parnassan plays). On this point see Hallett Smith, *Elizabethan Poetry* (Cambridge, Mass., 1952), p. 242; and Ejner Jensen, "Hall and Marston: the Role of the Satirist," *Satire Newsletter*, IV, no. 2 (1967), 72–83.

[19] *Historical Manuscripts Commission, Twelfth Report, Appendix, Part I: The Manuscripts of the Earl Cowper, K.G. Preserved at Melbourne Hall, Derbyshire*, Vol. I (London, 1881), p. 19.

same), translated into rollicking English by John Healy in 1609 as *The Discovery of a New World*. Just as the college students take a journey to "Parnassus" and then "return" to the world of reality, the traveler in *Mundus* (like a later Gulliver) voyages to four separate and very strange lands whose customs in drinking, eating, whoring, and governing themselves reflect upon those in England.

William Knight, who in 1605 edited and published *Mundus Alter et Idem* (the title page says "Frankfort"), wrote in his preface the following concerning Joseph Hall, the author:

Having long ago bid farewell to the Muses, to whom he had paid court with applause, and being wholly departed from them, he could never be tempted by no reward to allow his verses *and certain other inventions of his* [my italics], all most worthy of praise, to be put before the public gaze. Marry, he did use to say, as it were in order to excuse himself, that he had composed certain pieces in this kind [*huismodo*, i.e., in the kind of *Mundus Alter et Idem*] in his young days and leisure at the University for his own instruction and delight, but he declared it was fitting that he should dismiss them as bootless trifles, and he did stand upon this, that they should never appear to the public sight in his name.[20]

Surely William Knight in 1605 is not thinking of Hall's satires, which were published in his name; besides, Knight speaks of his verses and certain "other inventions." By "other inventions" could he mean "dramatic"? In the same breath he asserts that these "other inventions" were similar to the satirical, semi-bawdy, and "journeying" *Mundus Alter et Idem*. Does he mean the dramatic satires called "the Parnassan plays" which were put on at St. John's College? Hall's own introduction to *Mundus* is signed "*Peregrinus quondam Academicus*," in Healy's translation "The Cambridge Pilgrim." The phrase echoes the prologue of the last Parnassus play, "Making them Pilgrims to *Pernassus* hill." Who prevailed upon John Healy to leave out the "*quondam*"?

Why was the second *Returne from Parnassus* the only one of the three plays printed, twice in 1606? Obviously because it mentions Shakespeare, Jonson, and the "warriors of the theatres." It is also the best of the three plays. Could its publisher have received the manuscript from one of Hall's friends, Owen

---

[20] *Healy's The Discovery of a New World*, ed. and trans. Huntington Brown (Cambridge, Mass., 1937), Appendix B, pp. 142–143.

Gwynne of St. John's, perhaps, to whom the Stationers' Register assigns it, on condition that he respect Hall's wish to remain anonymous now that he was serving as rector in the parish of Sir Robert Drury and had just been asked by Lady Anne Drury's brother, Sir Edmund Bacon, to accompany him on a mission to the continent? [21] Cantabridgians must have known that just the year before, William Knight, possessing the manuscript of *Mundus*, had risked Hall's displeasure by publishing it in Hall's name and without Hall's permission.

We begin to draw to a close. Later in the century John Milton lashed out against the opponent of Smectymnuus, an able man of words whom he knew to be none other than Bishop Joseph Hall. In a context of making fun of Hall's *Mundus Alter et Idem*, Milton in 1642 wrote: "Let him go now and brand another man injuriously with the name of *Mime*, being himselfe the loosest and most extravagant *Mime*, that hath been heard of; whom no lesse than almost halfe the world could serve for stage roome to play the *Mime*." [22] In his own day at Cambridge Milton had seen with disgust divinity students play-acting in false beards and costumes. He almost puts himself back several college-generations in order to watch the young Joseph Hall of Emmanuel:

. . . that Playes must have bin seene, what difficulty was there in that? when in the Colleges so many of the young Divines, and those in next aptitude to Divinity have bin so oft upon the Stage writhing and unboning their clergie limmes to all the antick and dishonest gestures of Trinculo's, Buffons, and Bawds. . . . Judge now whether so many good text men were not sufficient to instruct me of false beards and Vizards without more expositors; . . .[23]

Forty years after the event, Milton is angry with this Anglican bishop for writing satires and a semi-bawdy *voyage imaginaire*, but also for something even worse, which Milton had evidently been told about: actually taking part at Cambridge in stage performances. One might expect such behavior in a St. John's or

[21] *The Returne from Parnassus* (second part) was assigned in the Stationers' Register, 16 Oct. 1605, to Owen Gwynn, Fellow of St. John's College and cousin to Richard Vaughan, Bishop of London from 1604 to 1607. See Miss Reyburn's article cited in note 3, above.

[22] "Apology against a Pamphlet" [The Yale] *Complete Prose Works*, Vol. I (1953), pp. 868–953, ed. Frederick L. Taft. This quotation comes from pp. 881–882.

[23] *Ibid.*, p. 887.

Peterhouse man but not in a Fellow at Emmanuel. As is well known, 1642 was the year of the "Puritan" closing of the theaters.

If the facts and suggested connections between these facts adduced in this paper can convince us that Joseph Hall is the major author of the second part of *The Returne from Parnassus*, then several other problems will fall into place: (1) why there are so many verbal parallels between the play and Hall's satires; (2) why Marston attacked Hall so vehemently; (3) what Hall's "other inventions" cited in 1605 were; (4) why Hall so resolutely turned his back on his literary beginnings; and (5) what justification Milton had in 1642 to use theatrical images against Hall while defending the Puritan pamphleteers.

If there were documentary proof, of course, there would be no need of a hypothesis. But the present hypothesis will stand until documentary proof is found, or until another hypothesis explains more of the facts than this one does.

II

REFLECTIONS AND
SELF-REFLECTIONS:

OUTLANDISH PROVERBS AS A CONTEXT FOR
GEORGE HERBERT'S OTHER WRITINGS

James Thorpe

I

Scholars of earlier literature sometimes express envy at the amount of material available to their fellows who undertake the study of more recent writers. To students of the more pristine—whatever the period of their interest—students of later ages seem blessed by a profusion of material, more varied in character than theirs, with fewer worrisome problems of text, with greater stores of biographical and historical information, and with less need to squeeze the evidence for the last drop of inference.

Those of us who are students of the major English nondramatic writers of the early and middle parts of the seventeenth century might remark the fact, for example, that none of our authors favored us by writing books about the writing of their books, as did Thomas Wolfe, William Gibson, Irving Wallace, and others. Nor do we have the vast stores of supportive and explanatory material that exists for later writers. There seem to be more than ten thousand individual letters still extant written by Charles Dickens, for example, and an equal number by John Ruskin. (The Huntington Library alone has about a thousand letters by each of them.)

On the other hand, our seventeenth-century authors wrote rather more literary works than we ordinarily reckon with. The sheer quantity of the writings of the major authors alone is rather remarkable, perhaps breathtaking. Imagine a shelf of the works of our authors in the Oxford English texts issued by the Clarendon Press. It is an impressive array of tall, thick books: Herbert and Herrick, Carew and Crashaw and Vaughan in one big, fat volume each; Lovelace and Marvell and Traherne each in two volumes, Donne in two if you are an ancient and many more if you are a modern. Milton, of course, deserves a full shelf, entirely to himself.

It is my impression that not many of us, even specialized students and scholars, bother with more than a small fraction of the works of these authors. I am not so visionary as to expect much conning of their writings in Greek and Latin, in which tongues the majority of them felt free to compose. One might, however, think it wise for the student of Herrick to be familiar with all 335 pages of his *Hesperides,* and even to have some acquaintance with the 65 pages of *His Noble Numbers,* in which "he sings the Birth of his Christ, and sighes for his *Saviours* suffering on the Crosse."

In my experience, it does not usually turn out that way. We gain our first knowledge of these writers from anthologies, our ideas become fixed, and most of us are content that our last knowledge of them is also a limited fraction of their total production. So it may properly be for connoisseurs of poetry, and may their tribe increase. The world is full of poems, more good poems than anyone can ever read. As lovers of poetry, we probably do well to accept traditional selections and pass on to something else, also good. Compromise always involves loss as well as gain, of course. The reader of Donne's poetry in even the most commodious selection, like Helen Gardner's *Metaphysical Poets,* will miss seven of the eight Satires, thirty-six of the thirty-eight Verse Letters, all twenty of the Epigrams, more than half of the Songs and Sonnets, both of his two most important poems—the two Anniversaries—and so on and so forth. But he may, instead, gain much from Spenser and Wordsworth and Yeats in the meantime.

I think that the scholarly student of Donne cannot afford such losses, though I readily admit that some scholarly books create the impression that their authors stopped reading poetry at a tender age. All scholarship is, I hope, an adventure in understanding. The understanding of any given poem involves, first and last, patient and careful reading with all the skill and knowledge that we can possibly bring to the poem. Beyond that—and

there is almost always something beyond that, for deep understanding—we must place the poem in one or another of its contexts. The context of genre, of convention, of form; the context
of social, cultural, intellectual history; the context of metrics,
language, and style; the context of literary movement and literary influence; and the like.

To put it simply but essentially, literary scholarship consists
in finding rewarding contexts for poems. (I am, of course, using
the word "poem" to stand for any literary work of art.) Contexts
are rewarding when they do such things as illuminate the poem,
make it more understandable, put it into just relationship with
other poems. Since everything is, in theory, a possible context for
a poem, it is a test of the scholar's tact in choosing—or, negatively, of his degree of pedantry—to see how comfortably the
poem fits in the context he has prepared for it, to observe how it
wishes to roost and nestle there. "All things have their place,"
says Herbert (Proverb 379), "knew wee how to place them."

My argument is going to be that one crucial context for the
poem is the other writings by the same author. I won't assert
that this is always the most important context of the poem, but
I think that it is more important than scholars commonly allow.
The business of criticism, so far as a given poem is concerned, is
to place it as an order of words within the context of all literature.
That is a rather large order, so far as I am concerned, and I cite it,
like Holy Writ, only to reassure you that we are proceeding under good auspices. It does seem within our powers, however, to
take the other writings of an author as a context for one or all
of his poems.

Today I want to turn this procedure around. I will take one of
George Herbert's prose works and see what kind of a context it
provides, in general or in particular, for his other writings or for
any other essences of his life, such as deep levels of his behavior.
This will be a kind of open inquiry, perhaps like that roaring lion
that walketh about, seeking whom he may devour. In any event,
I judge that almost any searching in the proverbs will be a nov-
elty for most people. At least, I cannot convince myself that they
have ever been read with attention by the very occasional writers
who comment on them, judging by the nature of their comments.

The work with which I wish to begin, and around which I
want my discourse to turn, is entitled *Outlandish Proverbs, Selected by Mr. G. H.* From there, I plan to talk a little about Her-

bert's English letters, and his prose work called *A Priest to the Temple*. These three constitute the major body of Herbert's prose. Finally, I will talk about some of the poems in *The Temple*. My intention throughout, however, is to work with the *Outlandish Proverbs* in the hope of finding, in them, a useful context for Herbert's other writings.

II

Herbert's *Outlandish Proverbs*—foreign proverbs, that is, not bizarre; there was no chauvinism in Herbert's makeup—number 1,032. He selected and translated them from various foreign sources, mostly from Italian, French, and Spanish. Very few had earlier appeared in English. Like almost all of Herbert's writings, the *Outlandish Proverbs* were not printed until after he died, in 1633; these first came out as a section of *Witts Recreation* (1640), with a separate title page. Several manuscript copies were made during his lifetime, including one (still extant, in the National Library of Wales) by his brother Sir Henry Herbert, and they were familiarly alluded to among his friends.[1]

Herbert's collection includes a few proverbs that most Americans know today, with only slight differences in phrasing. The first one in his collection—and perhaps it is symbolically significant that it stands first—is "Man Proposeth, God disposeth." Later comes "All is not gold that glisters" (306) and "Little pitchers have wide eares" (380). Also we find "In the kingdom of blind men the one ey'd is king" (469) and "The eye is bigger than the belly" (1018). There are a good many that are simply variant versions of familiar proverbs, like "In the house of a Fidler, all fiddle" (223), or "He that hath a head of waxe must not walke in the sunne" (425); "A penny spar'd is twice got" (506), and "A feather in hand is better than a bird in the ayre" (578).

I believe that the majority of Herbert's proverbs are relatively unfamiliar today, however, even though other versions are re-

---

[1] Long ago, doubt was expressed about Herbert's part in the *Outlandish Proverbs*. They were included by F. E. Hutchinson in *The Works of George Herbert* (Oxford, 1941) with evidence (pp. 568–573) that seems absolutely conclusive that Herbert selected and translated them. The enlarged version of the proverbs, published in *Herbert's Remains* (1652) under the title of *Jacula Prudentum*, adds some 152 proverbs; as there is no evidence to prove Herbert's part in this collection, I do not treat this version.

corded. Such as "Hee that wipes the childs nose, kisseth the mothers cheeke" (1032), or "Hee puls with a long rope, that waits for anothers death" (25). Many of these unfamiliar proverbs seem remarkably apt, like "He that commits a fault, thinkes every one speakes of it" (554), or "No barber shaves so close but another finds worke" (667), or again "When it thunders, the theefe becomes honest" (690). And I particularly commend this warm proverb: "If the mother had not beene in the oven, she had never sought her daughter there" (696).

If one were in search of a context for these proverbs, there would be many directions to take in order to place them in this popular genre. Their relations, for example, to the collections made by the great Renaissance humanists, like Erasmus; or to the collection prepared by Herbert's friend Francis Bacon; or to those included in Cotgrave's popular and influential *Dictionairie of the French and English Tongues* (1611); or to the Book of Proverbs in the Old Testament, with its extensive and elaborate Renaissance commentaries; or to the classical *sententiae;* or to the tradition of the aphorism, which most of us know from its brilliant flourishing in France later in the seventeenth century. Any of these lines of inquiry might lead to interesting results, for we are dealing with a genre that has had, despite its importance, surprisingly little scholarly attention.

As we have set ourselves a task which moves in the other direction, we might begin to seek for clues as to whether Herbert's proverbs are a context for his other writings by some elementary analysis of this collection. Consider, first, recurrences within the collection. The largest common denominator of the majority of the proverbs is their relevance to the ordinary conduct of ordinary human beings on ordinary occasions. The shy person is pushed forward with, "Manie things are lost for want of asking" (968). The imprudent man is advised, "Although it raine, throw not away thy watering pot" (325). The overadventuresome are told, "Praise the Sea, but keepe on land" (489). Those with ill tempers learn that "Soft and faire goes farr" (772). The perfectionists—like those who spend too long on their dissertations—hear that "Hee that makes a thing too fine, breakes it" (440). Those of us who may become discouraged receive special attention and numerous supports, such as "Hee begins to die, that quits his desires" (2), and "Every path hath a puddle" (215), and "One stroke fells not an oke" (181).

If we were to reconsider the entire collection in terms of imagery and substance, I feel sure we would find that the most common kind of imagery is related to country life, particularly to animals. Dogs have to carry a lot of proverbs on their backs. Such as "When a dog is a drowning, every one offers him drink" (77); or, "The scalded dog feares cold water" (13); or, a more familiar one, "He that lies with the dogs, riseth with fleas" (343). Many other animals appear in this pantheon. "The goate must browse where she is tyed" (56); or: "It's a bold mouse that nestles in the catts eare" (693). Not all is harmonious in the animal world, however: "The honey is sweet, but the Bee stings" (212). Moreover, the animal world is not always congenial for people: "Let not him that feares feathers come among wild-foule" (48).

The imagery of country life and animals is by far the most common. A poor second, as a source, derives from the business life of merchants and tradesmen. The miller, the blacksmith, the seller of any goods—all are prominent in these proverbs. It is interesting to notice what the usual point of view is: mostly the proverbs constitute advice or warning to the innocent buyer. Says one proverb: "The buyer needes a hundred eyes, the seller not one" (390). Another admonition runs this way: "On a good bargaine thinke twice" (529). Another says, "Ill ware is never cheape" (61). Once in a while the point of view is that of the detached commentator on the process of buying and selling, as in the observation, "He that blames would buy" (410).

There are two other topics that are frequently treated in the proverbs. One we can perhaps simply call religion, the other good physical health. It will not surprise many people, I imagine, to discover that God moves through a lot of Herbert's proverbs. A conventional consolation is offered in the proverb "He looseth nothing, that looseth not God" (35); and a fence against anxiety is erected by this one: "God sends cold according to Cloathes" (33). The role of providence is reiterated in the saying, "God heales, and the Physitian hath the thankes" (169). The fact that the providential role is not always tender is made plain in this warning, very useful for mothers with children who are finicky eaters: "Who likes not the drinke, God deprives him of bread" (394).

The large number of proverbs on health may be at first sight somewhat surprising, especially when one observes that the majority of them cluster around one very specific topic. That is, the importance for health of temperance in evening food and drink. "By suppers," we are told, "more have beene killed then

Galen ever cured" (272). I believe that it is not simply wine bib-
bing and luxurious cates that are being prohibited. "Hee wrongs
not an old man," says one proverb, "that steales his supper from
him" (311). Or, when it comes to drink, "Hee that goes to bed
thirsty riseth healthy" (1003). (And there are many others to
the same effect, like numbers 88, 93, 378, and 882.)

Let me conclude this brief analysis of the proverbs by mentioning three other rather special topics that loom important because of their recurrence. One is the importance of having a true
friend: such as "The best mirrour is an old friend" (296), or
"Life without a friend is death without a witnesse" (385). Another such recurrent topic is concern for children. One example
is this: "The best smell is bread, the best savour, salt, the best
love that of children" (741). A more vivid example is, "Better
a snotty child, then his nose wip'd off" (828). The last of the
special recurrent topics I will mention is dislike of talking too
much. Over and over again we read such observations as, "An
Oxe is taken by the horns, and a man by the tongue" (967). Or,
"Three can hold their peace, if two be away" (714).

III

On the basis of this very brief analysis of some of the more obvious features of the *Outlandish Proverbs*, I would like now to
inquire into some of the relations that they have to Herbert's
other works. I first consider his English letters, because they are
obviously personal and deeply sincere, with their import perfectly clear.

It came as something of a surprise to me to discover that almost
half of Herbert's letters in English contain remarks that resemble
proverbs. From Trinity College, Cambridge, he writes to his
stepfather, Sir John Danvers, saying: "Since your favours come
a Horse-back, there is reason, that my desires should go a-foot." [2]
It would be easy to convert this remark into a saying suitable,
both in substance and imagery, for inclusion in *Outlandish Proverbs*, like this: "When favours come a Horse-back, desires should
go a-foot."

Another letter to Danvers at almost the same time includes the

---

[2] *Works,* ed. Hutchinson, p. 363. All references to Herbert's works are to
this edition, by page number given in the text.

remark, "What Trades-man is there who will set up without his Tools?" (p. 364). This may remind us of Herbert's great fondness for proverbs using the imagery of tradesmen, and even suggest such an *Outlandish Proverb* as 67: "Never had ill workeman good tooles."

Let me just mention two or three other examples from his letters. To his brother, Henry Herbert, he writes: "it is the part of a poor spirit to undervalue himself and blush" (p. 366). His longest letter extant, written to his mother in 1622 in her serious illness, is full of proverb-like sayings, such as his observation of "the thred of Life to be like other threds or skenes of silk, full of snarles and incumbrances" (p. 373).

Or, finally, this passage from his letter of about 1630 to his brother now *Sir* Henry Herbert, Master of the Revels. It is a letter that shows his concern for children. The question was where the three orphaned daughters of his elder sister would live. Herbert's eldest brother Edward (Lord Herbert of Cherbury) had suggested that one of the two oldest go to George Herbert and his wife at Bemerton, but Herbert urges that the two oldest, close companions, be kept together and come to Bemerton; he also offers to take the youngest, despite his slender resources after having spent his money on repairing the Bemerton church. But to the passage:

Truly it grieves me to think of the child [the youngest one], how destitute she is, and that in this necessary time of education. For the time of breeding is the time of doing children good; and not as many who think they have done fairly, if they leave them a good portion after their decease. But take this rule, and it is an outlandish one, which I commend to you as being now a father, "the best-bredd child hath the best portion." Well; the good God bless you more and more; and all yours; and make your family, a housefull of God's servants (p. 376).

To repeat: *Take this rule, and it is an outlandish one . . .* "*the best-bredd child hath the best portion.*" This proverb, which Herbert puts in quotation marks, is number 953 in his *Outlandish Proverbs:* "The best bred have the best portion." Notice also that he calls it "this rule," from which we can understand that he took this proverb—and, proverbs generally, I imagine—as pieces of essential wisdom, as rules of behavior, in the way that the Jews understood the teachings of the "wisdom" books in the Old Testament, like the book of Proverbs. Proverbs had various uses, in Herbert's view, but he apparently did not think of them as opportunities for the display of rhetorical cleverness or wit.

IV

Now I turn to *A Priest to the Temple*, which bears the subtitle of *The Countrey Parson His Character, and Rule of Holy Life*. I believe that most people do not realize the double meaning in this title of the term "The Temple," a double meaning which also applies to Herbert's title for his poems. "The Temple" is a place for the worship of God, a special church; but it is also the soul of man. In Herbert's letter to his mother in her illness, he talks of the soul and says: "Consider that God intends that to be as a *sacred Temple* for himself to dwell in" (p. 374). So both the Priest and the collection of Herbert's poems relate both to the Church as a place of worship and to the human soul as the habitation of God. Herbert says of the Priest that "the greatest and hardest preparation is within" (p. 226). I believe it is the preparation of the human soul that is Herbert's greatest, hardest, and ultimate objective.

This prose work, *A Priest to the Temple*, commonly called by its subtitle, *The Country Parson*, consists of thirty-seven chapters and two concluding sample prayers. It was not printed until 1652, almost twenty years after Herbert's death, when an acquaintance arranged for its publication. Herbert had left it quite complete, however; the first edition even includes a signed preface entitled "The Authour to the Reader."

It is plain from the Preface that he wrote the book for his own instruction. "I have resolved to set down the Form and Character of a true Pastour," he writes, "that I may have a Mark to aim at: which also I will set as high as I can" (p. 224). *The Country Parson* is Herbert's own "Mark to aim at" himself, but it is for others as well; he asks that "the Lord prosper the intention to my selfe, and others, who may not despise my poor labours, but add to those points, which I have observed, untill the book grow to a compleat Pastorall" (p. 224)—that is, a fully realized book relating to the cure of souls.

Herbert applied to this book such terms as "Rule" (in the subtitle), "Mark" (in the Preface), and "Aim" ("Now Love is his business, and aime" [p. 284]). His suggestion as to how the Parson should preach on his texts ("of Devotion, not Controversie, moving and ravishing texts") could describe *The Country Parson*; we are to proceed "by dipping, and seasoning all our words and sentences in our hearts, before they come into our mouths, truly affecting, and cordially expressing all that we say; so that the auditors may plainly perceive that every word is hart-deep" (p. 233).

One way to get into the substance of *The Country Parson* is through its imagery. Take a single chapter, Chapter IV, "The Parson's Knowledg," and look at the beginning, the middle, and the end (pp. 228–229). "The Countrey Parson is full of all knowledg," it begins. "They say, it is an ill mason that refuseth any stone: and there is no knowledge, but, in a skilfull hand, serves either positively as it is, or else to illustrate some other knowledge. He condescends even to the knowledge of tillage, and pastorage, and makes great use of them in teaching, because people by what they understand, are best led to what they understand not." Thus the beginning. The middle, as I see it, is this sentence: "The second means is prayer, which if it be necessary even in temporall things, how much more in things of another world, where the well is deep, and we have nothing of our selves to draw with." The end is this sentence: "Wherefore he hath one Comment at least upon every book of Scripture, and ploughing with this, and his own meditations, he enters into the secrets of God treasured in the holy Scripture."

The common imagery is, of course, husbandry: for the beginning, the analogy of the mason and the stone; for the middle, drawing water out of a well; and for the end, ploughing. This use of imagery applies to the principle that "people by what they understand, are best led to what they understand not."

But also notice the form of the first statement. "They say, it is an ill Mason that refuseth any stone." This is the form of a proverb, even identified as such by the characteristic introduction, "They say." Herbert uses a close version of the same proverb in his poem called "The Church-Porch": "The cunning workman never doth refuse / The meanest tool that he may chance to use" (p. 20). A close version of Herbert's proverb had appeared in Cotgrave in 1611 ("The cunning mason workes with any stone") and in one modern collection.[3]

Herbert uses a number of his *Outlandish Proverbs* in *The*

<hr>

[3] See M. P. Tilley, *A Dictionary of the Proverbs in England in the Sixteenth and Seventeenth Centuries* (Ann Arbor, 1950), M 707.

Country Parson. To start with a familiar one: in telling what the Country Parson should do "in providing a stock for his children," Herbert says that "good deeds, and good breeding, are his two great stocks for his children" (p. 240). We will recall Herbert's letter to his brother on the same point, and remember that this is another adaptation of proverb 953, "The best bred have the best portion." (Also see Tilley, B 648 for other versions and examples.)

On the very same page in *The Country Parson*, he delights to think that his wife, his children, and his servants will all be the beginners of good discourses, to good effect. "As in the house of those that are skill'd in Musick," he says, "all are Musicians; so in the house of a Preacher, all are preachers." The *Outlandish Proverb* being used here is number 223: "In the house of a Fidler, all fiddle." (Also see Tilley, H 777.)

In the chapter called "The Parson in Journey" we hear what the Parson does when he stops overnight at an Inn. He returns thanks for his safe arrival, says grace at meat, offers prayers in the hall before retiring, asking the host to invite the other travelers to join him. "The like he doth in the morning," continues the text, "using pleasantly the outlandish proverb, that *Prayers and Provender never hinder journey*" (p. 251). The proverb is number 277 in Herbert's collection, where it reads, "Prayers and provender hinder no journey." (Also see Tilley, P 556.)

In the chapter of advice to the Parson as to how he should behave in order to avoid contempt—"that generall ignominy which is cast upon the profession"—first comes a "holy and unblameable life." Next, "a courteous carriage, & winning behaviour." Why? "He that wil be respected, must respect" (p. 268). This statement is the positive version of *Outlandish Proverbs* 427: "Hee that respects not, is not respected." (Also see Tilley, R 86.)

The chapter on "The Parson's Surveys" is mainly an outline of how to cope with idleness, which is described as "the great and nationall sin of this Land." The Parson goes about his parish, surveying the faults. The chapter offers positive suggestions to help different sorts of people to avoid idleness. The landed gentleman, for example, might, after attending to his family, look to "the improvement of his grounds, by drowning, or draining, or stocking, or fencing, and ordering his land to the best advantage both of himself, and his neighbours. The *Italian* says, None fouls his hands in his own businesse" (p. 275). The formula "The *Italian* says" is a signal that a proverb is coming, and so it was.

It is number 419 in *Outlandish Proverbs*, and perhaps clearer there than in *The Country Parson:* "Who doth his owne businesse, foules not his hands." (See also Tilley, B 755.)

In addition to these various passages which can be traced to the *Outlandish Proverbs*, there are many other passages in *The Country Parson* that are in the general form of proverbs. Let me only refer to a few examples. In the Preface, Herbert lays it down that "hee shoots higher that threatens the moon, then hee that aims at a Tree" (p. 224). The same proverb appears in Sidney's *Arcadia*, and is recorded in modern dictionaries of proverbs.[4] Later, Herbert cautions the Parson against excess drinking in the company of others, as he will afterward find it impossible to reprove them for other faults. Then comes the proverb: "For sins make all equall, whom they finde together" (p. 227). One final example. The Parson should try to avoid contempt. For which reason, one wonders. The answer is put in the form of a proverb: "Where contempt is, there is no room for instruction" (p. 268).

If we take *The Country Parson* as a whole, it can serve, I think, as a certain form of spiritual autobiography. It is different, in many ways, from the contributions to this genre by Dissenters, such as Bunyan's *Grace Abounding to the Chief of Sinners*. Herbert's book is soul-oriented, but at the same time it is behavior-oriented. It achieves its cast, in some important measure, through the frequent reliance on proverbs as a mode of setting "rules" or "marks" or "aims" for human behavior.

V

Finally, we come to talk of Herbert's poetry, substantially all of which he assembled in a manuscript collection under the title of *The Temple*; its subtitle is *Sacred Poems and Private Ejaculations*. It is, I believe, one of that small group of truly great books of poems. Like the other things I have spoken of, it was published posthumously, but within the year of his death. In his final illness, he sent the manuscript to his friend Nicholas Ferrar to read through and decide whether to have it published or burned. Izaak Walton gives a dramatized account of this transaction, but it certainly embodies the kind of truth that yields the right sense

---

[4] *Oxford Dictionary of English Proverbs*, 3d ed. (Oxford, 1970), p. 726; Tilley, M 1115.

of Herbert's view of his own poems. Herbert is made to say that the poems are "a picture of the many spiritual Conflicts that have past betwixt God and my Soul." If Ferrar thinks that the collection "may turn to the advantage of any dejected poor Soul, let it be made publick; if not, let him burn it." [5] Both of these comments are important guides to an understanding of Herbert's poetry. As to the nature of his poetry, "a picture of the many spiritual Conflicts that have past betwixt God and my Soul," as *The Country Parson* is in some sense another picture of his own spiritual life, capable of being read from the outside in, with the poems capable of being read from the inside out. As to the intent in making his poetry public, if it "may turn to the advantage of any dejected poor Soul," as *The Country Parson* is in some sense an effort to set "a Mark to aim at," a "rule," an "aim" for the advantage of any other person committed to the cure of souls.

When I begin reading Herbert's poems in the light of what I have been saying about proverbs and purpose, I see several things that I had never before noticed.

First, that a few of the poems embody proverbs that are simply taken over from *Outlandish Proverbs*. In "Confession," we read that God's afflictions "fall, like rheumes, upon the tendrest parts." This is Proverb 475, "Wealth is like rheume, it falles on the weakest parts." In the poem entitled "A Dialogue-Antheme," Death says "Let losers talk." Proverb 602 reads "Give loosers leave to talke," and the same proverb is recorded in modern reference books with many early citations.[6] In "The Glimpse"—which is, I think, a much better poem than it is reckoned—the heart quells fears at possible loss of delight by saying, "A slender thread a gentle guest will tie." This is Proverb 726, "A gentle heart is tyed with an easie thread."

Next, I notice that a few poems embody expressions which have all the characteristics that one expects of proverbs, but which are not (so far as I have discovered) either in *Outlandish Proverbs* or recorded in the usual reference books. For example, the last line of "Repentance" concludes the poem with this flourish: "Fractures well cur'd make us more strong"—which does just about everything a proverb can do except be recorded as a proverb. "The Church-Porch" has this proverb-like warning, "Slacknesse breeds worms" (l. 339). One poem, "Charms and

---

[5] *The Life of Mr. George Herbert* (London, 1670), p. 109. The account is unchanged in the 1675 edition of Walton's *Lives*.

[6] *Oxford Dictionary of English Proverbs*, p. 485; Tilley, L 458.

Knots," devotes all of its eighteen lines to proverbs, two lines to a proverb: such as, "Who reade a chapter when they rise, / Shall ne're be troubled with ill eyes"; or "Who shuts his hand, hath lost his gold: / Who opens it, hath it twice told."

Finally, I notice that a great many of Herbert's poems include passages that are reminiscent of proverbs. They are not proverbs but they are what we might call "convertible passages"—passages that could, without very much effort, be converted into proverbs. Consider, as one example, the conclusion to "Easterwings": "For, if I imp my wing on thine, / Affliction shall advance the flight in me." Affliction helps us, as fractures are said to make us more strong. "H. Baptisme (I)" concludes with the couplet that "What ever future sinnes should me miscall, / Your first acquaintance might discredit all"; it is the thought that "first acquaintance discredits all" which has a proverbial ring. Similarly, the ending of "The H. Scriptures. II" lays it down that "Starres are poore bookes, & oftentimes do misse: / This book of starres lights to eternall blisse"—the entire couplet is a convertible passage, especially the first part of it. As a last example, let me mention the end of "H. Baptisme (II)": "The growth of flesh is but a blister: / Childhood is health"—"childhood is health." I could mention a very large number of further examples, but I will spare the reader.[7]

VI

I would really prefer not to offer a formal conclusion to this inquiry. Not out of timidity or laziness, I hope, but in the thought that each of my readers will know, better than I can, where and how far a certain structure of ideas moves him in his own attitudes. Moreover, it is a far better fortune to set the occasion, even unwittingly, on which a person creates an idea that fits him than to press upon him a series of thoughts that were cut to another's pattern.

But let me venture to offer some tentative hints about one or two things that I think I am learning along these lines. I hope that these hints will be understood as the specific application of the principle of contexts. There would, I trust, be other values

---

[7] Here are some further examples: "Jordan (II)," last two lines; "Faith," ll. 27–28, 29–30; "Love I," ll. 9, 13–14; "Constancie," l. 24; "Sunday," l. 33; "The Discharge," l. 10.

and other hints—not contradictory but amplifying—from attending to other contexts for Herbert, and this or other contexts for other writers.

I began by suggesting that we may take one work, Herbert's *Outlandish Proverbs*, and see what kind of context it provides for some of his other works. When I center my attention on that work and then read Herbert's other writings, I notice—for the first time, for me—how much Herbert is given to the use of proverbs all through his other writings. Some passages seem precisely in the form of proverbs, but much more often there is a pervasive tone that is reminiscent of the lore and style of proverbs.

As it turns out, I am not much interested in the details for their own sake, of how one of Herbert's works influenced another, nor whether he used the same expression more than once. I might be if I were a glossing editor, but fortunately I am not. I am interested in the cast of mind that is revealed. I am interested in the type of inner consistency which is suggested by the kinds of recurrences and analogies that appear. And I am interested in recognizing that a common purpose animates his works of very different character. Together, these make up an important context.

The context which the *Outlandish Proverbs* offers for Herbert's other writings helps me to clarify in my own mind how essentially he was concerned with ordinary human behavior, how he longed to have marks and aims that would be useful for himself and for others, how his mind ran toward understandable imagery that could aid understanding. It was for these reasons and in these ways—as I am coming to realize—that he offered the embodiments of his spiritual conflicts, which are his poems, to our attention.

CONTROLLING IDEAS

III

TYPOLOGY AND POETRY:
A CONSIDERATION OF HERBERT,
VAUGHAN, AND MARVELL

Barbara K. Lewalski

The elaborate system of interrelated meanings and symbolic significances produced by many centuries of typological exegesis of the Scriptures created a resource for poetic allusion and symbolic reference which was still important for art and poetry in the sixteenth and seventeenth centuries. I propose to explore certain literary uses of typology in seventeenth-century poetry, focusing upon George Herbert's *The Temple*, Henry Vaughan's *Silex Scintillans*, and Andrew Marvell's *Upon Appleton House*.[1] In this inquiry my concern is not with typology as an arcane system of thought, but rather with its literary uses and permutations —with what it provided to poets who sought to interpret man's religious and historical experience, and what they made of what it provided.

To begin with, we should recognize that the medieval exegetical principles which created typology as a fully developed hermeneutical system received during the Protestant Reformation some significant changes in emphasis. The basic medieval formula, enunciated by Augustine and repeated constantly, recognized a literal or historical meaning of Scripture residing in the signification of the words and, in addition, a spiritual meaning

[1] All texts of poems are taken from the following editions: *The Works of George Herbert*, ed. F. E. Hutchinson (Oxford, 1959); *The Complete Poetry of Henry Vaughan*, ed. French Fogle (New York, 1964); *The Poems and Letters of Andrew Marvell*, ed. H. M. Margoliouth, 2 vols. (Oxford, 1967).

whereby the things or events signified by the words point beyond themselves to other things or events.[2] Aquinas's classic account of the so-called fourfold method of exegesis recognized in addition to the literal meaning three spiritual senses of Scripture: allegorical (meaning in this special usage typological) in which persons and events in the Old Testament prefigure Christ and various events in the New Testament, and sometimes prefigure also the Christian Church as Body of Christ; tropological or moral, in which what our Head Christ has done is an example of what we ought to do; and anagogical, in which Old and New Testament events prefigure the end of time or "eternal glory." [3] The general term "allegory" was commonly understood to involve the use of fictions or contrived sequences of signs which are not true or real in themselves but refer or point to underlying spiritual truths. The typological process by contrast is a pattern of signification in which type and antitype, as historically real entities with independent meaning and validity, form patterns of prefiguration, recapitulation, and fulfillment by reason of God's providential control of history.[4]

As everyone knows, the cardinal principle of Protestant hermeneutics was the "one sense of scripture," the sole authority of the literal meaning. But while this Reformation rallying cry was used to discount allegorical interpretations imposed wholesale on the text of Scripture, it did not overturn the accepted system of typological relationships, especially those that were understood to have Evangelical or Pauline warrant: the ceremonies of the Law as a "shadow of things to come," the rock struck by Moses as a type of Christ, Adam and the various Old Testament patriarchs as types of Christ. But there were differences of emphasis, arising from the Protestant understanding of typological symbolism as a part or dimension of the literal meaning rather than as a distinct spiritual sense.

For one thing, Protestants revised the common medieval conception of Old Testament personages and events as merely literal signs or shadows pointing toward New Testament truth or spiritual reality, asserting rather that they also embody, though less

[2] Augustine, *De Doctrina Christiana* I.2 (no. 2), II.15 (nos. 23–24), III.6 (nos. 10–20), trans. D. W. Robertson, Jr. (Indianapolis and New York, 1958), pp. 8–9, 50–51, 84–92.

[3] Thomas Aquinas, *Summa Theologica* I. Q.I., Art. 10, *Basic Writings of Saint Thomas Aquinas*, ed. Anton C. Pegis, 2 vols. (New York, 1945).

[4] For this distinction see, e.g., Erich Auerbach, *Mimesis*, trans. Willard Trask (Princeton, 1953), pp. 63–66, 170–176.

fully, the spiritual meaning of the New Testament antitype. In this vein, instead of interpreting the Old Testament manna and circumcision as literal signs prefiguring the Christian sacraments, Calvin insisted that these also were genuine sacraments, and that "those promises that were geven unto them, did so shadow and prefigure the Gospell, that they did include the same within them selves." [5] This emphasis permitted Protestants to identify their own spiritual experience much more closely with that of the Old Testament types than medieval exegetes customarily did, and to regard history as a continuum rather than as two eras of time divided by the Incarnation of Christ.

Related to this, Protestant exegetes modified the medieval focus upon Christ's life and death as the primary antitype fulfilling the Old Testament types *forma perfectior* by emphasizing instead the contemporary Christian as antitype, recapitulating in himself the experiences recorded in the Old and also the New Testament. This application of Scripture to the individual is akin to what medieval exegetes called the tropological or moral sense—"so far as the things done in Christ, or so far as the things which signify Christ, are signs of what we ought to do." [6] But the Protestants' sense of the desperate condition of fallen man led them to shift the emphasis from *quid agas* to God's activity, and so to assimilate the pattern of individual lives to the pervasive typological patterns discerned in biblical and later Christian history. In this spirit John Donne in his sermons characteristically explicated Scripture texts and events in terms of their recapitulation in himself and his hearers—"a repeating againe in us, of that which God had done before to Israel, or . . . a performing of that in us, which God promised by way of Prophesie to Israel." [7]

I

George Herbert's book of religious poetry, *The Temple*, was published posthumously in 1633. Although Rosemond Tuve's fine book on Herbert has demonstrated the importance of typology to the imagery and argument of many lyrics,[8] her essentially

---

[5] Calvin, *A Commentarie upon S. Paules Epistles to the Corinthians*, trans. Thomas Tymme (London, 1577), fols. 116v–117.

[6] Aquinas, *Summa Theologica* I. Q.I., Art. 10, *Basic Writings*, I, 17.

[7] *The Sermons of John Donne*, ed. Evelyn M. Simpson and George R. Potter, 10 vols. (Berkeley and Los Angeles, 1953–1962), III, 313.

[8] *A Reading of George Herbert* (Chicago, 1965).

medieval perspective does not take account of the Protestant emphasis throughout the volume upon the spiritual experience of the individual Christian as an antitype of the Old Testament types. Nor, I suggest, has typological symbolism been properly applied to the vexed question of the work's artistic unity—the interrelationship of the three large subsections of *The Temple*—*Church-Porch, The Church*, and *Church Militant*—as well as of the 166 lyrics that comprise the dominant central section, *The Church*.

The poem, "The Bunch of Grapes," affords the most explicit statement of Herbert's conception of typology as God's own symbolism, inherent in the nature of things and in the providential history recorded in his Word. The poem could easily have been an emblem poem, a poetic complement to an engraving of the large cluster of grapes brought back by Joshua's spies from the Promised Land of Canaan as a foretaste of its riches—but no emblem poem we know has anything like this poem's complexity. Although the poem depends for its meaning upon our recognition of the traditional typological relationship between the grapes hanging from the pole carried by the spies and Christ on the cross, the true vine pressed in the winepress of the Passion (Isaiah 63:3) to become the wine of the New Covenant, what is most significant about Herbert's use of typology in this poem and throughout *The Church* is, first, his presentation of contemporary Christians as a direct antitype of the Israelites:

> For as the Jews of old by *Gods* command
>   Travell'd, and saw no town;
> So now each *Christian* hath his journeys spann'd:
>   Their storie pennes and sets us down.
> A single deed is small renown.
> Gods works are wide, and let in future times;
> His ancient justice overflows our crimes.
>
>   [8–14]

Beyond that, however, and also wholly characteristic of the method of *The Church*, is the location of the entire typological relationship in the heart of the speaker. The poem is not fundamentally about the Old Covenant and the New as type and antitype, but rather about the speaker's loss of spiritual joy and content. Exploring this, he finds that his spiritual life recapitulates the experience of the Israelites wandering in the desert, but that unlike them he is given no tangible earnest or assurance of the

Promised Land. The resolution comes as the speaker apprehends that Christ's redemptive sacrifice is a more significant part of his spiritual experience, and that this sacrifice affords a less tangible but far more certain and all-embracing guarantee of spiritual joy.

The first poem in the collection of lyrics entitled *The Church* is the pattern poem "The Altar"; its fundamental typological terms extend to and unify the diverse lyrics in that collection. On their surface, the various lyrics suggest various aspects of the life of Christian man in the Church, but in fact the true subject of all these poems is the church in the heart of man. All aspects of church architecture, church liturgy, and the entire historical experience of the people of God are caught up in and recapitulated in this speaker—who is a kind of Christian everyman to be sure, but also a particular Christian poet and priest. In "The Altar" this speaker and the poetic record of his spiritual experience is made the primary antitype of all the types, in that his heart, not the New Testament church altar, is the direct antitype of the altar of unhewn stones which figures so prominently in the divine prescriptions for the altar of sacrifice in the Old Testament:

The Altar.

A broken A L T A R, Lord, thy servant reares,
Made of a heart, and cemented with teares:
  Whose parts are as thy hand did frame;
  No workmans tool hath touch'd the same:
     A H E A R T alone
     Is   such   a   stone
     As   nothing   but
     Thy pow'r doth cut.
     Wherefore each part
     Of my hard heart
     Meets in this frame,
     To praise thy Name:
That, if I chance to hold my peace,
These stones to praise thee may not cease.
O let thy blessed S A C R I F I C E be mine,
And sanctifie this A L T A R to be thine.

God's directive to the Israelites wandering in the wilderness (Exod. 20:24–25) called for the altar of sacrifice to be made of unhewn stone, "for if thou lift up thy tool upon it, thou hast polluted it." This directive was repeated for the building of the more permanent tabernacle in the Promised Land, and also for the altar in Solomon's Temple. Protestant commentators commonly associated with these texts God's promise (Jeremiah 31:33) of a new covenant written in the heart of man superseding the law written in tables of stone; his promise in Ezekiel 11:19–20, "I will take the stony heart out of their flesh, and will give them an heart of flesh"; and also his declaration in Isaiah 66:1–2 that he does not dwell in houses built by men's hands but (alluding to Psalm 51) with the man "that is poor and of a contrite spirit." Protestant exegetes found in this medley of passages a foreshadowing of Christian worship under the New Covenant, and also of the new tabernacle and new altar in the regenerate man's heart. The proof texts were 1 Corinthians 3:9, 16, "Ye are God's husbandry, ye are God's building. . . . Know ye not that yee are the temple of God, and that the Spirit of God dwelleth in you," and also 1 Peter 2:5, "Ye also, as lively stones, are built up a spiritual house, an holy priesthood, to offer up spiritual sacrifices, acceptable to God by Jesus Christ." [9]

In "The Altar" Herbert alludes to all these places, and to the conventional relationship of type and antitype which they present. His interpretation of them with specific reference to the human heart receives elucidation from a comment by Joseph Hall:

Every renewed man is the individual temple of God. . . . What is the Altar whereon our sacrifices of prayer and praises are offered to the Almighty, but a contrite heart? . . . Behold, if *Solomon* built a Temple unto thee, thou hast built a Temple unto thy selfe in us. We are not only through thy grace living stones in thy Temple, but living Temples in thy Sion. . . . Let the Altars of our cleane hearts send up ever to thee the sweetest perfumed smoake of our holy meditations, and faithfull prayers, and cheerfull thanks-givings.[10]

In his poem "The Altar" Herbert's speaker makes these theological ideas radically personal, presenting himself as the antitype of the Old Testament altar, his own heart as the altar which

[9] For Protestant comment see, e.g., annotations on these verses in the Geneva Bible (*The Bible: That is, the Holy Scriptures* [London, 1597]); in Franciscus Junius and Immanuel Tremellius, *Biblia Sacra* (London, 1593); in Henry Ainsworth, *Annotations upon the Five Books of Moses, the Booke of the Psalmes, and The Song of Songs* (London, 1627); in Andrew Willet, *Hexapla in Exodum: That is, A Sixfold Commentary upon the Second Booke of Moses Called Exodus* (London, 1608); and in Lancelot Andrewes, *XCVI Sermons*, 4th ed. (London, 1641), pp. 445–492.

[10] Joseph Hall, *Contemplations upon the Principall Passages of the Holy Storie* (London, 1642), pp. 1158–1159.

must be hewn by God, himself as the Church of the New Covenant which must be built by God, not man. This, I suggest, is the perspective that unifies the various categories of lyrics that comprise *The Church*, as can perhaps be indicated by even a cursory account of these categories.

Following "The Altar," the first group of poems works out the theological basis for the speaker's formation as the New Church—his acceptance of, and relation to, Christ's sacrifice. To begin with, Christ, the speaker of the poem "The Sacrifice," delivers an irony-charged indictment of men's ungrateful and inept responses to His passion and crucifixion. In the next several poems—"The Thanksgiving," "The Reprisall," "The Sinner," "Good Friday"—the speaker of the rest of the lyrics learns that it is fruitless to try to match or imitate by his own good works the passion of Christ, but that he can only accept the overwhelming gift as the true sacrifice to be offered on the altar of his stony heart. Concluding this theological sequence is another pattern poem, "Easter-wings," which shows the speaker now ready and eager to "imp my wing" on Christ's rising, thereby advancing his own flight by his very sins and afflictions.

Other categories of poems, thematically related but not presented sequentially, internalize other dimensions of the church. One group concerns the architecture and furniture of the church —"The Church-floore," "The Windows," "Church-musick," "Church-monuments"—all of which elements are then identified as aspects of the speaker's religious life: his virtues, his responsibility to preach the Word, his exaltation by music, his meditations. Again, God is proclaimed as the only builder of the church in the heart: "Blest be the *Architect*, whose art / Could build so strong in a weak heart" ("The Church-floore," ll. 19–20). Yet another body of poems concerns liturgical feasts or ceremonies, also located in the speaker's heart: "Whitsunday" invokes the Spirit to "spread thy golden wings in me / Hatching my tender heart"; "Trinitie-Sunday" celebrates in triplets the action of each member of the Trinity upon the heart; "Christmas" finds the speaker attempting to match the shepherds in their song for Christ's birth. Still another category of poems, of which "The Bunch of Grapes" is an example, interprets the speaker's religious experience as a recapitulation of certain scriptural types and their antitypical fulfillments, thereby locating biblical history as well within the individual; others of this kind are "Josephs coat," "Aaron," and "Sion."

The final and largest category of poems, with titles such as "Miserie," "Affliction," "Man," "Giddinesse," "Confession," "The Pulley," "The Collar," "A True Hymne," "Mortification," seems difficult at first to relate to the controlling typological symbol of the temple in the heart, though they do conform to Herbert's description of his collection of lyrics as "a picture of the many spiritual Conflicts that have past betwixt God and my Soul." [11] The opening poem, "The Altar," also provides the appropriate frame of reference for these poems, as well as the terms for relating them to Herbert's unifying conception, by means of the allusion to Psalm 51:15–17:

> O Lord, open thou my lips; and my mouth shall shew forth thy praise.
> For thou desirest not sacrifice; else I would give it: thou delightest not in burnt offering.
> The sacrifices of God are a broken spirit: a broken and a contrite heart, O God, thou wilt not despise.

The speaker of "The Altar" activates the conventional Protestant conception of David the Psalmist as a figure for the entire range of Christian spiritual experience, recording, as Donne put it, "what I, what any shall doe, and suffer, and say." [12] Medieval commentators usually interpreted the Psalms as prefiguring Christ himself or Christ living in His members (His Church), [13] but Protestant accounts emphasize rather the recapitulation of David's spiritual experience in any and every Christian individual. Calvin declared, "I have been accustomed to call this book [The Psalms], I think not inappropriately, 'An Anatomy of all the Parts of the Soul'; for there is not an emotion of which any one can be conscious that is not here represented as is a mirror." [14] Calvin also affords Herbert's speaker a precedent for taking the events of his own particular life as a recapitulation of the experience of David and the other patriarchs recorded in the Psalms: "It tends greatly to lighten grief, to consider that . . . we are

---

[11] Izaak Walton, *The Lives of John Donne, Sir Henry Wotton, Richard Hooker, George Herbert, and Robert Sanderson*, 4th ed., 1675 (Oxford, 1956), p. 314.

[12] Donne, *Sermons* VII, 51. See Ben Jonson, *Underwood*, no. I, ll. 7–16, for a close analogue to Herbert's use of the allusion to Psalm 51:15–17.

[13] See, e.g., St. Augustine, *Expositions on the Book of Psalms*, trans. J. Tweed et al., 6 vols. (Oxford, 1847); *The Holie Bible*, 2 vols. (Douai, 1609), II, 1–12.

[14] John Calvin, *Commentary on the Book of Psalms*, trans. James Anderson, 5 vols. (Edinburgh, 1845), I, Preface, xxxvi–xxxvii.

just called to engage in the same conflicts with which David and the other Holy patriarchs were exercised." And again, "It has greatly aided me [to know] . . . that I had suffered the same . . . things from the domestic enemies of the Church." [15] Luther's perspective in his *Manual of the Book of Psalms* is even more suggestive for Herbert's speaker, in that he considered the range of experiences treated in the Psalms to extend to the entire Church, but at the same time to be located in every Christian individual:

The Book of Psalms [collects] . . . the feelings and experiences of all the faithful, both under their sorrows and under their joys, both in their adversity and their prosperity. . . . When thou findest thyself under the same feelings that David was; when the chords and strings of his harp are really re-echoed by the feelings and sensations of thy heart; thou mayest assure thyself that thou art in the congregation of the elect of God. . . . Take the Psalms into thy hands; this will be as an all-clear mirror, which will represent to thee the whole church in its true features; and if thou be one that fears God, it will present to thee a true picture of thyself.[16]

Such commentary affords the basis for Herbert's unifying idea. Although David had not been permitted to build up the Old Testament Temple (his son Solomon did that), yet the Psalmist did present the type of the broken and contrite heart which must be the center, the altar, of the New Covenant church. Moreover, the echoes in "The Altar" from Psalm 51 and from Luke 19:40, "I tell you that, if these should hold their peace, the stones would immediately cry out," together with the motto from Herbert's title page, "In his Temple doth every man speak of his honor," connect the building of the temple in the heart which must be God's work only, with the raising in that temple of appropriate praises to God. Here also Calvin's commentary is suggestive:

He [David] prays that *his lips may be opened;* in other words, that God would afford him matter of praise. The meaning usually attached to the expression is, that God would so direct his tongue by

---

[15] *Ibid.*, I, 134, Preface, xxxix–xl. Cf. Theodore Beza, *The Psalmes of David*, trans. Anthonie Gilbie (London, 1581); George Wither, *A Preparation to the Psalter* (London, 1619); R[ichard] B[ernard], *David's Musick: Or Psalmes of that Royall Prophet* (London, 1616).

[16] Martin Luther, *A Manual of the Book of Psalms*, trans. Henry Cole (London, 1837), pp. 5, 10–11.

the Spirit as to fit him for singing his praises. But though it is true that God must supply us with words, and that if he do not, we cannot fail to be silent in his praise, David seems rather to intimate that his mouth must be shut until God called him to the exercise of thanksgiving by extending pardon.[17]

In making this connection, Herbert seems to have been the first major poet to conceive his chief work, in general outline and in detail, as a direct response to the suggestion implicit in Calvin, Sidney, Puttenham, Donne, Milton, and many others, that David's Psalms should be taken as archetype and model for Christian lyric poetry.[18]

Not only has Herbert conceived his book of lyrics, *The Church*, as a contemporary recapitulation of David's Book of Psalms in the sense that it records the full range of a Christian's spiritual experience, but he has also incorporated into his book the various generic and rhetorical kinds commonly assumed to be contained in the Psalms. It was customary to discover in the Psalms the three kinds of lyrics Paul enumerated in Ephesians 5:19 as appropriate to Christian use—psalms, hymns, and spiritual songs.[19] A further discrimination of kinds was often made on the basis of the titles given to various psalms, as George Wither indicates in his *Preparation to the Psalter* (1619):

The Names of the *Psalmes* are many: such as these, *A Psalme; A Song; A Hymne; A Prayer; Instructions; Remembrances; Of Degrees; Halleluiah*, or *Praises*. . . . By a *Psalme*, the Auncient Expositors understood such verses as being composed in the honour or praise of some Subject, were indifferently intended, to be either read or sung; as are our ordinary English Sonnets, consisting of fourteene lines. A *Song* was made of *Measures*, composed purposely to be sung. *Hymnes* were Songs in which were the praises of God onely,

---

[17] Calvin, *Commentary on . . . Psalms*, II, 303.

[18] Calvin, *Commentary on . . . Psalms*, I, xxxviii–xxxix; Sidney, *The Defence of Poesie* (1595), Scolar Press facsimile (Menston, 1971), sigs. C1v–C2; George Puttenham, *The Arte of English Poesie* (1589), Scolar Press facsimile (Menston, 1968), p. 23; Donne, *Sermons* II, 49, V, 288–89; Donne, "Upon the Translation of the Psalmes by Sir Philip Sidney and the Countesse of Pembroke," in *Divine Poems*, ed. Helen Gardner (Oxford, 1959), pp. 33–35; Milton, *The Reason of Church Government*, in *Complete Prose Works*, Vol. I, ed. Don M. Wolfe (New Haven, 1953), pp. 815–816. Cf. Lily B. Campbell, *Divine Poetry and Drama in Sixteenth Century England* (Cambridge, Eng., 1959), pp. 20–54.

[19] See, e.g., Henry Ainsworth, *Annotations upon the Booke of Psalms* (London, 1626), sig. R4.

and that with joy and triumph; . . . those that are intituled *Halle-luiah*, are *Hymns* also, mentioning particularly the praises of God for benefits received. Now of what nature they are which be called *Prayers, Psalms of Instruction*, or such like, the very names of some of them doe plainely enough declare.[20]

It was also conventional to observe that all these kinds were as-similated to the overarching purpose and category of praises of God, as the very name of the Book of Psalms in Hebrew, *Sepher Tehillim*, testifies.[21]

Anyone familiar with the range of lyrics in *The Church* will recognize how apt these categories are for the kinds there in-cluded: fifteen sonnets and numerous sonnet-like poems, pray-ers, instructions, meditations, praises, songs, antiphons, hymns; he will also recognize that the whole of *The Church* is con-cerned with praise of God. Prominent in developing this theme of praise is the poem "Easter" which analyzes the poetic process of devising divine praises. The heart must first experience the occasion within itself—"Rise heart; thy Lord is risen." The lute, or poetic talent, must then "struggle" for its part. But the Holy Spirit must make a third in order to produce the fit song—which then follows. The two "Jordan" poems invoke the typological relationship between the Israelites' crossing Jordan to the Prom-ised Land and Christian Baptism in describing the baptism of the poet's verse to God's service—and again the poet discovers that his method and manner of praising must be from God. And in that later, very moving poem, "The Forerunners," the poet con-fronts and then resolves the problem of age and waning poetic powers by echoing Psalm 31:14 in his refrain, "Thou art still my God." Identifying these words as his only necessary poetic state-ment, he recognizes fully that God's power, not his own, is the source of the praises emanating from the temple built in the heart, even as it is of that temple itself.

Typological formulations also provide a basis for the thematic and structural unity of the whole collection—the relation of the long prefatory poem, *The Church-Porch*, and the long epilogue, *The Church Militant*, to the central body of lyrics, *The Church*. Criticism of Herbert has pointed to the traditional typological significance of the three parts of the Old Testament Temple— the Porch typifying the external and visible aspect of the church

[20] Wither, *Preparation to the Psalter*, p. 54.
[21] *Ibid.*, p. 44; Donne, *Sermons* V, 270; IX, 350.

from which none are excluded, the Holy Place typifying the communion of the invisible church on earth, and the Holy of Holies typifying the highest heaven of the saints; alternatively, in Daniel Featley's terms, the three parts typify the states of Nature, Grace, and Glory. Critics have often tried to fit Herbert's work to these terms as to a Procrustean bed.[22] It seems obvious that Herbert has made some use of these conventional typological associations in the conception of the first two sections of his work, *The Church-Porch* and *The Church*. His application of these terms, however, is rather to the Christian individual than to the ecclesiastical body, in a formulation similar to that of Joseph Hall: "In every renewed man, the individual temple of God, the outward parts are allowed common to God and the world, the inwardest and secretest which is the heart, is reserved onely for the God that made it . . . onely the true Christian hath intire and private conversation with the holy One of Israel." [23] Accordingly, in Herbert's *Church-Porch* the speaker sets forth a series of dry, didactic prescriptions regarding the externals of the Christian life and the behavior fitting a Christian profession which constantly echo classical moral philosophy and ethics. The precepts have affinity both with the Church and with the world, even as the church porch as an architectural metaphor is seen to have associations both with the Old Testament Temple Porch and with classical pagan temples, for both kinds of temples have contributed directly to the definition of the external moral behavior appropriate to the Christian life, although both are but shadowy types of the Christian temple in the heart. The lyrics of *The Church* define that Christian temple itself, the inner essence of the Christian experience, as the relationship between Christ and the individual soul and the distresses and joys attendant upon that relationship.

But the equation does not hold for the third term: Herbert's *Church Militant* cannot be made to relate to the Holy of Holies in the Old Testament Temple, or to its antitype, the heavenly

---

[22] See, e.g., John D. Walker, "The Architectonics of George Herbert's *The Temple*," *ELH*, xxix (1962), 289–305; Mary Ellen Rickey, *Utmost Art: Complexity in the Verse of George Herbert* (Lexington, Ky., 1966). The traditional typological equations are set forth in Thomas Adams, "The Temple," *Works* (London, 1629), pp. 980–981; Willet, *Hexapla in Exodum*, p. 629; Daniel Featley, "The Arke under the Curtaines" (1613), *Clavis Mystica* (London, 1636), p. 576.
[23] Hall, *Contemplations, Works*, p. 1158.

kingdom. Indeed, Herbert suggests the soul's movement into that third realm at the end of *The Church*, in a series of poems on the last things—"Death," "Dooms-day," "Judgement," "Heaven"—followed by the final exquisite lyric, "Love III," which intimates the soul's gracious reception at the heavenly banquet. For *The Church Militant* the significant terms are set forth by the extended opening passage about the Ark—both Noah's Ark and more importantly the Ark of the Covenant—and also by allusions throughout the poem to the fleeing woman of the Apocalypse, all of which were recognized types of the Church Militant in its relation to the world. Daniel Featley's comment seems almost a précis of Herbert's poem: "The Spouse of Christ [is] a pilgrime, and flieth from place to place, from Citie to Citie, from Kingdome to Kingdome. . . . The Portable Arke in the Old Testament, and the flying woman in the New, are images of the militant Church in this world." [24] Herbert's *Church Militant* develops just such a vision of the Church traveling ever westward as Sin dogs her heels, destroying or taking over the communities she has established, until at length the Lord comes to judge both the Church and the World. Herbert's perception is that the Temple, with its intimations of permanence, has its true antitype only in the hearts of the elect who look forward to individual salvation, but that the wandering Ark is the nearest type for the corporate body of the Church, which has no security here and is (as Augustine also saw) in constant conflict with the world. Herbert's overarching typological symbol, the Temple, is then an appropriate ground of unity for his entire work, foreshadowing in different ways the three dimensions of the New Covenant church. The prefatory poem, *Church-Porch*, explores the external behavior proper to the Christian man; the dominant central section, *The Church*, presents the intimate spiritual experience of the regenerate heart; and the epilogue, *The Church Militant*, is again concerned with an external dimension, the constant tribulations of the visible church in this world, typified by the wandering Ark which is itself a foreshadowing of the more permanent Temple.

[24] Daniel Featley, "The Embleme of the Church Militant," in *Clavis Mystica*, p. 300. Cf. Robert Cawdray, *A Treasurie or Store-House of Similes* (London, 1600), pp. 93–94, "As the Arke was carried from place to place, and never rested in one certaine place: So likewise the militant Church here on earth, hath no certaine place, but is posted from piller to post."

II

Henry Vaughan's volume of religious lyrics, *Silex Scintillans*, was first published in a complete edition in 1655.[25] In it Vaughan testifies by countless imitations and echoes as well as by direct statement that Herbert's example was largely responsible for making him a religious man and a religious poet. Like Herbert, Vaughan makes impressive use of typological symbolism, and he carries further the distinctively Protestant emphasis upon the contemporary Christian as an antitype of the Old Testament types. The poem "White Sunday" affirms this general typological principle:

> Besides, thy method with thy own,
> Thy own dear people pens our times,
> Our stories are in theirs set down
> And penalties spread to our Crimes.
>
> [29–32]

"Man's fall, and Recovery" underscores the spiritual advantages that the New Covenant provides to the contemporary Christian, so that he fulfills the types *forma perfectior:*

> This makes me span
> My fathers journeys, and in one faire step
> O're all their pilgrimage, and labours leap,
> For God (made man)
> Reduc'd th'Extent of works of faith; so made
> Of their *Red Sea,* a *Spring;* I wash, they wade.
>
> [27–32]

Moreover, Vaughan imitated Herbert's special poetic formulation of this Protestant typological principle, making the speaker of his poems the locus of both Old Testament and New Testament experience. An example is "The Law, and The Gospell," in which the speaker sets forth the conventional type-antitype relation between Mount Sinai and Mount Sion, and then asks that both be embodied in himself: "O plant in me thy *Gospel*, and thy *Law*, / Both *Faith*, and *Awe*" (ll. 27–28).

But despite these resemblances to Herbert and to certain gen-

25 Part One was published separately in 1650.

eral tendencies in Protestant typological commentary, Vaughan uses typological symbolism in distinctive and individual ways, confirming in this area also the justice of Joan Bennett's observation that "Herbert may have made Vaughan a poet, but he did not make him in his own image." [26] For Vaughan typological allusion is not so pervasive as with Herbert, nor does it afford the impressive thematic and structural unity that Herbert was able to attain through his dominant metaphor of the speaker's heart as New Covenant temple or altar. Vaughan's prefatory emblem of the flashing flint striking a stony heart and also some references in the dedicatory poems suggest that he might originally have intended this focus, but he develops instead—in part through typological allusion—the metaphor of the Christian pilgrimage. This metaphor provides considerable thematic and tonal unity to the volume as a whole, and reinforces the loosely articulated structural links relating Part I and Part II of *Silex*. Vaughan's speaker is often a pilgrim wandering through a natural or a biblical landscape (usually a conflation of both), thereby recapitulating as an antitype the wanderings of the Old Testament patriarchs as well as the "way" of Christ described in the New Testament.[27] In the poem "Religion" the pilgrim speaker finds himself walking about in the same groves where Elijah, Zachariah, Gideon, Ishmael, Jacob, Abraham, and other Old Testament patriarchs encountered angels, or else heard in fire or whirlwind or still small voice the pronouncements of God himself. Attributing the disruption of such conference in modern times to the ever-increasing corruption in the once pure "Spring" of religion, he calls upon Christ to cleanse these waters anew, recapitulating the bib-

---

[26] Joan Bennett, *Five Metaphysical Poets* (Cambridge, Eng., 1966), p. 85. See Preface to *Silex Scintillans*, Part II, "The first, that with any effectual success attempted a diversion of this foul and overflowing stream, was the blessed man, Mr. *George Herbert*, whose holy *life* and *verse* gained many pious *Converts* (of whom I am the least)."

[27] The Pilgrim metaphor was central to Reformation conceptions of the Christian life and experience. The principal biblical sources are: Hebrews 11:13–16, "These [Old Testament Fathers] all died in faith, not having received the promises, but having seen them afar off . . . and confessed that they were strangers and pilgrims on the earth. . . . But now they desire a better country, that is a heavenly"; Hebrews 12:1, "let us run with patience the race that is set before us"; Hebrews 13:14, "For here have we no continuing city, but we seek one to come"; 1 Peter 2:11, "I beseech you as strangers and pilgrims, abstain from fleshly lusts." For typical exegesis, see commentary on these texts in the Geneva Bible (1597); in John Diodati, *Pious and Learned Annotations upon the Holy Bible* (London, 1648), and in John Calvin, *A Commentarie on the Whole Epistle to the Hebrewes,* trans. C. Cotton (London, 1605).

lical types—the sweetening of the bitter waters of Marah, the creation of water from the Rock by Moses' rod, the change of water to wine at the wedding feast. In the following poem, "The Search," the pilgrim speaker searches the New Testament biblical landscape where the notable events of Christ's life took place, in an effort to find and follow Christ, but a singing voice tells him that the true antitype of these events and places lies in the universe within the self or in the heavenly world to come: "Search well another world; who studies this, / Travels in Clouds, seeks *Manna*, where none is" (ll. 95–96).

Vaughan may be differentiated from Herbert also in that he accentuates the Protestant tendency to blur the distinctions between Old and New Covenant spiritual experience. The poem "Religion" shows the speaker's religious life to be only potentially an antitype *forma perfectior* of that the patriarchs; actually, the progressive decay and corruption of religion places him in many respects on a lower plane, though he may look forward to the glorious fulfillment of the New Covenant promises at the end of time. This ambiguity finds most complete expression in the poem, "The Retreate," in which the speaker longs to undertake a reverse pilgrimage so as to "travell back" to the early days of his "Angell-infancy," a condition that is conflated with that "ancient track" from whence could be seen the "shady City of Palm Trees"—Jericho, the promised land and type of heaven. The end of the pilgrimage is here fused with the beginning as the speaker prays to return "in that state I came." Because of this paradox, when Vaughan's speaker relates himself specifically to certain Old Testament types in defining his pilgrimage, he often seems to recapitulate their experiences simply, rather than to fulfill them, *forma perfectior*.

One special type for the speaker is Israel wandering in the desert. In "Joy of My Life" he identifies God's saints as his own Pillar-fire like unto that which guided the Israelites, and in "Psalm 121" he finds the conventional antitype, Christ, to be his Pillar and Cloud. In the opening lines of "The Mutinie"— "Weary of this same Clay, and straw"—he sees himself recapitulating the situation of Israel enslaved at the brick kilns of Egypt, and later he too is wandering in the wilderness. Recapitulating also the Israelites' murmurs against God, he observes that God has "a shorter Cut / To bring me home, than through a wilderness, / A Sea, or Sands, and Serpents" (ll. 29–31), but yet he affirms his desire to follow obediently whatever path God has devised for him.

Alternatively, the speaker is often in the situation of Jacob, who set forth for Laban's country "on foot, in poor estate" as Henry Ainsworth explains, with only his staff in his hand.[28] In the poem "Regeneration" the speaker finds himself suddenly in a fresh field—"Some call'd it, Jacobs Bed" (l. 28)—where Jacob slept on a stone and dreamed of the ladder reaching to heaven, and where he later anointed the stone as an altar to God. In "Religion," and "The Search" the speaker finds himself at Jacob's Well but desires instead its antitypical fulfillment, Christ the Fountain of Living Waters offered to the Samaritan woman (John 4:1–14). In "The Pilgrimage" he finds himself lodged like Jacob in some nameless place but dreaming of heaven, and he prays to be maintained like another Elijah with sustenance enough to travel to the Lord's Mount. In "Jacobs Pillow, and Pillar" the speaker finds Jacob's simple stone pillar to be a type of the Church of the New Testament located in the hearts of the faithful, and he finds Jacob's struggles with his brother to be recapitulated in the turmoils of the English Civil War; but he perceives also that the comfort afforded by Jacob's stone pillow is far surpassed by its antitype which he enjoys, Christ.

Finally, the speaker often identifies himself with Ishmael, the firstborn of Abraham by the bondmaid Hagar, who was cast out with his mother onto the desert so that he might not inherit with Isaac, the chosen seed. Regarding Ishmael as a type of the reprobate, medieval exegetes attributed to natural providence alone the sending of God's angel to direct Hagar to a fountain so that she might fill the bottle of the weeping, thirst-wracked Ishmael.[29] Yet many Protestants, most notably Luther, saw Ishmael as a type of the gentiles who were to become heirs to the promise, and interpreted God's providential act as a foreshadowing of the grace to be offered to them:

[28] See commentary on Genesis 28:5–22, 32:10, in Henry Ainsworth, *Annotations upon the Five Bookes of Moses*, etc., pp. 105–107. For other discussions of Jacob as Pilgrim, see Thomas Playfere, *The Whole Sermons* (London, 1623), pp. 112–113; Thomas Gataker, "Jacobs Thankfulnes to God, for Gods Goodnes to Jacob: A Meditation on Genesis 32:10," *Certaine Sermons* (London, 1637), p. 297.

[29] See commentary on Genesis 21:9–21 in Douai Bible; on Galatians 4:22–26 in *Glossa Ordinaria, Patrologiae Cursus Competus, Series Latina*, ed. J. P. Migne, 221 vols. (Paris, 1844–1864), vol. 114, cols. 580–81.

The account could not have been written in a more horrifying way
. . . death is imminent for both, and from thirst at that, which is
unbearable for our nature. . . . the mother is so heartbroken for
grief that she cannot bear the sight of her dying son. . . . But even
though Ishmael is cast out of the house and the Church of Abraham
. . . I do not doubt that Ishmael and many of his descendents were
converted to the church of Abraham. For the expulsion does not
mean that Ishmael should be utterly excluded from the kingdom of
God. No, the purpose is to let him know that the kingdom of God
is not owed to him by reason of a natural right, but comes out of
pure grace. . . . After he had been crushed in this manner, he simply renounced his right. Later on he came into the inheritance as a
guest, as Paul says about the Gentiles in the Epistle to the Ephesians.
[2:11–12] [30]

On this understanding, the speaker's sense of himself as recapitulating the situation of the weeping Ishmael is less surprising: in
"The Timber" he prays that on his way through the desert his
bottle may be filled with the tears of his repentance; in "Begging
II" he complains of God's coldness to his cries whereas of old
"thou didst hear the weeping lad"; in "Providence" he cites the
story of Ishmael's rescue as type of the providential care he expects of God; and in "The Seed growing secretly" he cries out as
a new Ishmael for the dew of grace from heaven: "O fill his bottle! thy childe weeps" (l. 16).

Remarkably, Vaughan intersperses such typological allusions
with frequent references to and echoes of the Song of Solomon,
which both Medieval and Reformation exegetes interpreted in
allegorical rather than typological terms. That is, this book was
read as a poetic fiction whose true meaning concerned the relation of Christ with the Church or with the Christian soul, and
not as the literal history of Solomon and his bride which pre-
figured those relationships. But whereas exegetes in the Roman
Catholic tradition tended to interpret the allegory concerning
Christ and the individual soul as a paradigm of the contemplative
life or the mystical experience,[31] most English Protestant commentators (e.g., Richard Sibbes, Henry Ainsworth, George

[30] Luther, *Works*, ed. Jaroslav Pelikan, Vol. IV (St. Louis, Mo., 1964), pp.
41–43. See also *Geneva Bible* (1597), annotations on Galatians 4:22–31.
[31] See, e.g., Origen, *The Song of Songs, Commentary and Homilies*, trans.
and annotated by R. R. Lawson (London, 1957); François de Sales, *The Mystical Explanation of the Canticle of Canticles* (1643), trans. Henry B. Mackay
(London, 1908), Vol. VI.

Gyfford, John Dove)[32] saw it as a paradigm of the typical Christian life from the time of effective calling or regeneration—"Draw me, we will run after thee"—through the uneven course of spiritual triumphs and failures which mark the process of sanctification, to a settled condition of longing for and earnest expectation of the Second Coming. As John Robotham put it, "The Song began with a desire of the kisses of Christs mouth, so . . . concludes also with a desire of his comming in glory."[33] Through numerous epigraphs, references, and imagistic echoes, Vaughan's speaker invokes the Song of Solomon to help define his own Christian pilgrimage, reading its allegorical significance in his own historical experience, even as he elsewhere presents his experience in typological terms, as an antitype of several Old Testament pilgrimages. Vaughan employs both the allegorical and the typological mode, then, to embody in a particular individual (the speaker) certain biblical paradigms having the same symbolic import—the Christian pilgrimage.

"Regeneration," the first poem in the collection following the dedicatory verses, prepares us for this mixture of symbolic modes as well as for the motifs that unify Part I of the volume as a treatment of the beginning phases of the Christian pilgrimage with their attendant vicissitudes. As has been noted, when the speaker of this poem is brought suddenly to "a faire, fresh field" called Jacob's Bed—the place Bethel where Jacob slept on a stone pillow and had his vision of the ladder leading to heaven—the reference functions typologically in that the speaker here recapitulates Jacob's experience. Yet this reference is contained within the more pervasive allegorical mode of the poem, presenting the speaker's experience of regeneration as a fictional journey. As "A Ward, and still in bonds," the speaker went walking one day upon a primrose path in a false spring, but then perceived that his interior climate was wintry, that the spring was "Meere stage, and show," and that he was a pilgrim in a monstrous, mountainous landscape enduring wintry rains. Climbing to the mountaintop he found a pair of scales, which showed him that the pains

[32] Richard Sibbes, *Bowels Opened: Or, a Discovery of the Neare and Deare Love, Union and Communion Betwixt Christ, and the Church, and consequently betwixt Him and every beleeving Soule* (London, 1641); Henry Ainsworth, *Solomons Song of Songs* (London, 1623); George Gyfford, *Fifteene Sermons upon the Song of Solomon* (London, 1598); John Dove, *The Conversion of Solomon* (London, 1613).

[33] John Robotham, *An Exposition on the whole Booke of Solomons Song, Commonly called the Canticles* (London, 1651), p. 772.

of his climb were far outweighed by the "smoake, and pleasures" of his sins and follies. At this some cried "Away" and he fled to the "faire, fresh field" that is Jacob's Bed, where he entered a lovely, springtime grove with azure sky, shining sun, garlands of flowers, spicy air, a murmuring fountain with a cistern full of stones (some lively and some dormant), a bank of flowers with some buds open to the sun and some closed, and a rushing wind proclaiming its intention to blow "where I please." The basis for the imagery and progression of the poem derives from conventional Protestant exegesis of the Song of Solomon 2:10–12, "Rise up, my love, my fair one, and come away. / For, lo, the winter is past, the rain is over and gone; / The flowers appear on the earth; the time of the singing of birds is come; and the voice of the turtle is heard in our land." George Gyfford's sermon upon this passage explains much of Vaughan's allegory:

The allegorie . . . is taken from the times of the yeare. . . . And that is, what the state of all the elect was before their calling: and then what it is after they be called of the Lord and regenerate. Before they be called, their hearts bee even like the earth in winter, under the colde frost and stormes of sinne; for there can be no sweete thing grow up, there is an utter barrenness. After that the Lord hath called them, and that they be regenerate, there is an heavenly warmth of his spirit, and the sweete dew of his graces, and then sweet flowers appeare, and then the holesome fruites doe bud forth: then is there peace and joy in the Holy Ghost, even heavenly melodie, which is represented heere by the singing of the birds.[34]

Other exegetes understood the winter season to apply specifically to "the menaces and showring threats of the Law" as John Robotham put it, and the subsequent spring to the Gospel Covenant;[35] this meaning is adumbrated in "Regeneration" by the speaker's situation as a ward, and by the balance scales on the mountaintop (Sinai, evidently) which reveal graphically the ineffectuality of the speaker's works, so that he is warned away from this mountain even as was another pilgrim by a character named Evangelist in another Pilgrim's Progress. In Jacob's Bed, Bethel, the garden of the Church watered by the Living Fountain which is Christ and his word, the speaker finds that grace alone makes some flowers bloom and some stones lively (in 1

[34] Gyfford, Fifteene Sermons, pp. 79–80.
[35] Robotham, An Exposition, p. 345. See also Henoch Clapham, Three Partes of Solomon His Song of Songs Expounded (London, 1603), pp. 153–154.

Peter 2:5 the faithful are termed "lively stones"). The poem's epigraph, "Arise O North, and come thou South-wind, and blow upon my garden, that the spices therof may flow out," is based upon Song of Songs 4:16, glossed by Protestants as a reference to God's unconditioned grace distributed "where I please," and also to the soul's need for both the purgative north wind and the refreshing south wind of grace to produce the fruits of sanctification.[36]

Subsequent poems—"The Holy Communion," "The Sap," "The Proffer," "Fair and Yong Light"—continue the presentation of the speaker's spiritual experience as a specific historical embodiment of the allegory of the Song of Songs. In "Dressing" he explores his need of purgation by reference to the purity demanded by the Bridegroom as "he feedeth among the lillies" (Song of Solomon 2:16), and this motif is intensified in "Cock-Crowing" as the speaker begs for the removal in eternity of his veil of mortality and corruption, but also pleads for the indulgence of the Bridegroom's continued presence despite his earthly impurity—"O take it off! or till it flee, / Though with no Lilie, stay with me" (ll. 47–48). In "The Night" the two modes are again intertwined. The lines, "When my Lords head is fill'd with dew, and all / His locks are wet with the clear drops of night" (ll. 32–33), carry an allusion to the Song of Solomon 5:2, "I sleep, but my heart waketh: it is the voice of my beloved that knocketh, saying, Open to me, my sister, my love, my dove, my undefiled: for my head is filled with dew, and my locks with the drops of the night." The passage was usually glossed as a reference to the somnolence produced in the soul by the care of worldly things, and to her awakening as Christ calls and sheds upon her the dew of grace won in the night of his earthly life and passion.[37] The speaker finds this allegorical experience given concrete realization in his own life, but he invokes typology also in this poem, for he finds himself recapitulating the experience of Nicodemus who sought and found the divine light in Christ by night, hidden though it was by the flesh and by the darkness of general unbelief: "Wise *Nicodemus* saw such light / As made him know his God by night" (ll. 5–6).[38]

[36] See, e.g., Robotham, *An Exposition*, pp. 512–522; Gyfford, *Fifteene Sermons*, pp. 103–104.
[37] See, e.g., Ainsworth, *Solomon's Song of Songs*, Annotations on Song of Solomon 5:2.
[38] John 3:21.

A further range of symbolic allusion in *Silex Scintillans* is supplied by the Book of Revelation and other biblical references to the end of time. These references are chiefly in the typological mode, for the speaker looks forward to the Apocalypse as the great antitype fulfilling all the types with which he had associated himself. This emphasis upon the apocalypse as antitype (rather than upon Christ's incarnate life and passion) is a distinctively Protestant tendency in exegesis which Vaughan carries much further than Herbert did. In poem after poem— "Church Service," "Burial," "The Dawning," "They are all gone into the world of light!" "The Day of Judgement," "The Throne," "The Feast"—Vaughan projects by epigraph and imagery the apocalyptic fulfillment of present experience. These references receive special emphasis in "Ascension-day" which, as the first poem in Part II of *Silex Scintillans*, sets forth the unifying motifs that are to predominate in Part II. The speaker finds that the biblical event of Christ's ascension is recapitulated in himself, raising him to a new plane of spiritual assurance above the worldly vicissitudes and turmoils of Part I:

> Thy glorious, bright Ascension (though remov'd
> So many Ages from me) is so prov'd
> And by thy Spirit seal'd to me, that I
> Feel me a sharer in thy victory.
>   I soar and rise
>   Up to the skies,
>   Leaving the world their day,
>   And in my flight,
>   For the true light
>   Go seeking all the way.
>
> [5–14]

The allusion made by the angels at Christ's ascension to his return in glory ("This same Jesus, which is taken from you into heaven, shall so come in like manner" [Acts 1:11]) provided the basis for viewing the episode as a type of Christ's Second Coming, and that typological symbolism is involved at the end of this poem as the speaker echoes John's plea to Christ at the end of the Book of Revelation to "come quickly." Apocalyptic reference is also important to the lyrics of Part II as a whole, for in them the speaker's expectation of, and longing for, the Apocalypse are deeply intensified. In the final poem, "L'Envoy," the speaker imagines the Second Coming with great vividness and immediacy—"Arise, arise! / And like old cloaths fold up these skies, / This long worn veyl: then shine and spread / Thy own bright self over each head" (ll. 7–10)—but yet the poem and the volume end with the speaker's affirmation of his willingness to wait here with patience until the number of the saints should be completed.

III

Marvell's *Upon Appleton House,* probably written in 1651, is a very different kind of work from either of those treated, emerging as it does from the classical and contemporary generic tradition of the topographical panegyric or country-house poem. This work also is often said to lack unity, and indeed, as Rosalie Colie has demonstrated in her recent book, a certain brokenness and multiplicity of perspectives is central to the poem's art.[39] I suggest, however, that the elements are made to coalesce into some overarching unity primarily through Marvell's version of typological symbolism. Marvell's poem is concerned with praise of the Fairfaxes rather than praise of God, but this secular praise is nevertheless conceived in Christian metaphysical terms, such that a particular estate (Fairfax's Nunappleton) and a real event (the retirement of the general Thomas, Lord Fairfax, and his family to that estate to escape the moral dilemmas of the English Civil War) are made the basis for exploring the realm of nature, pristine and corrupted, and the realm of nature restored, that is, of grace.

In his use of the typological mode Marvell intensifies the distinctively Protestant emphasis noted in Herbert and especially Vaughan and, more remarkably, transfers that mode from the realm of devotional poetry to that of secular history. In essence, Marvell assimilates the history of the Fairfax family and the topographical features of the Fairfax estate, as well as the experiences of the speaker who is making a progress around the estate, to the course of providential history, by showing both speaker and family recapitulating certain biblical situations. They are not antitypes, however, as the speaker of devotional poetry may be when he records the spiritual privileges he enjoys through the New Covenant, for the personages and events in secular history

[39] *My Ecchoing Song: Andrew Marvell's Poetry of Criticism* (Princeton, N.J., 1970).

cannot normally be said to present a higher order of spiritual reality than the biblical paradigm. Yet the mode may still be termed typological, for the contemporary recapitulations Marvell treats—of the Edenic state, of the Fall, of the wilderness experience with its temptations and wanton destructions, of the Flood with its chaotic disintegration—are seen to be divinely ordered by a Providence which has designed the repetition of the historical experience of the Israelites in that of God's chosen Englishmen. *Appleton House* thus builds upon and extends into the public realm the Protestant conception of history as a continuum rather than as two eras of time divided by the Incarnation, as well as the Protestant sense of the repetition of biblical events in the lives of contemporary Christians.

These recapitulations are most obvious in that history of the Fairfax family which the speaker narrates at the outset of his progress through the estate. His account begins with the tale of a fair and lovely virgin tempted by wily deceivers (the nuns), seduced by them to break faith with her intended betrothed (Sir William Fairfax), and to dwell with them in a convent characterized by perversions of both nature and religion. She is rescued from captivity by her intended bridegroom with whom she establishes a family—an act that restores the estate to the good purposes of nature and also reforms religion: "Twas no *Religious House* till now" (l. 281). This true history recapitulates and fuses, in a conflation characteristically Marvellian, the event of mankind's first fall through the seduction of Eve by the serpent, and her (our) rescue by the Bridegroom, the Second Adam; and also the corruption of nature and religion in the English nation by popery and their restoration in the Protestant Reformation.

The topographical characteristics of the estate are also assimilated to this pattern of recapitulations. The estate itself bears some intimations of Eden, but in fact images the social order which regenerate man is able to impose upon a fallen world.[40] The house is "natural" and humble, fitted to the dimensions of the human body, and its narrow door affords practice for entering into "Heavens Gate"; its "Frontispiece of Poor" and "Furniture of Friends" display the physical and spiritual support and nourishment which it affords to the larger social community. The

[40] There is something of this range of significance in Ben Jonson's *Penshurst* also, but in that estate the adumbrations of the Edenic condition and of the Golden Age are seen to be in stasis, fixed and firm, not located in and affected by the historical process, as they so manifestly are at Nunappleton.

adjacent garden Thomas Fairfax planted, with its ordered regiments of flowers and volleys of sweet perfume, more nearly adumbrates the Edenic condition. Yet the fortress character of the garden, the martial formation of the flowers, and the gardening efforts directed to the weeding of ambition and the tilling of conscience emphasize again that this is the possible garden state after the Fall—which demands a constant readiness for defensive Christian warfare in relation to the five senses, as well as a posture of self-defense toward external threats. The speaker then questions whether such a garden state could be maintained in the nation as a whole: England itself was once the "Paradise" of the four Seas where "All the Garrisons were Flowrs" (l. 332), but war-torn, ravaged England where decisions must be made about overturning and executing monarchs is no garden for tilling conscience. Yet it remains an open question whether Fairfax ought not to have continued his efforts in the national garden:

> And yet their walks one on the Sod
> Who, had it pleased him and *God*
> Might once have made our Garden spring
> Fresh as his own and flourishing.
>
> [345–349]

In the meadow below the garden ("the Abbyss . . . / Of that unfathomable Grass" ll. 369–370), the speaker and his audience view a kaleidoscope of harvest scenes which are emblematic of, and are conflated with, the bloody events of the English Civil War—the mowing of the grain (all flesh is grass); the sometimes unintentional and sometimes wanton destruction of the creatures living in the grass, high and low alike; the harvest maids turning their pitchforks on the quick rails and preparing greedily to sup on them; the harvesting of the grain which seems like a pillaging. These scenes are further conflated with and shown to recapitulate the Exodus story, with the Israelites affording a paradigm (reiterated in the English Puritans and emblematized in the mowers) of the ambivalent condition of sinful man in the wilderness, pressing forward to whatever happens to be the current version of the promised land, in the wake of divine miracles and human wrongdoings. The harvest scenes ring changes on all these ambiguities in the Israelites' story—their miraculous passage through the Red Sea (destroying all their pursuers); their slaughter and pillaging of the Pagan tribes (at their Lord's behest); their continued lusting for the flesh and delicacies they had enjoyed in Egypt—desires that God both satisfied and punished by a rain of quails. In this meadow, "Rails rain for Quails, for Manna Dew" (l. 408).[41] The meadow next appears as a razed, harvested plain which "*Levellers* take Pattern at" (l. 451) —recapitulating the bare earth before God began the creation of animal life; it is then flooded, with all things in it topsy-turvy, emblematizing the disorder in nature and society produced by war (whether Israelite or English) and echoing also the utter chaos produced by Noah's flood.

From this Chaos / Flood the speaker takes refuge in the "Sanctuary of the Wood" which he describes as his "green, yet growing Ark" (l. 481), his version of Noah's Ark which was a type of the Church as agent of man's salvation. The speaker's Ark / Sanctuary is also a means of salvation, holding a "mystic" key to all the histories the speaker knows and all the events in his experience, if he can but read it in the "light *Mosaick*" (l. 582)— the reference is both to the "various light" refracted by nature and the inspired light by which Moses wrote of the first creation and the natural order before the Fall. What the woods present are emblems of order in nature: the stock doves are emblems of marital harmony and society; the herons pay appropriate tribute to man as their Lord; the hewel fells hollow oaks but leaves sound ones untouched and further enacts natural justice by destroying the "traitor worm" within the oak—and in nature (if not in England) the royal oak itself seems content to fall, as if aware of its own hollow condition and satisfied that justice is done to the worm.

The speaker attempts a complete fusion with this natural landscape, hoping to be separated wholly from the corrupt world and kept "safe." He becomes completely passive, supposing himself an "inverted tree," and languishing with ease on the velvet moss. But this is no permanent solution for him or for us, because he is not pure and just like a tree or a hewel. Accordingly, his fantasy of violent imprisonment and crucifixion whereby he urges nature to restrain him by force from the world's evils reminds us that only through another crucifixion, above nature, can man and the human world be restored:

---

[41] See Numbers 9, and the discussion in John M. Wallace, *Destiny his Choice: The Loyalism of Andrew Marvell* (London, 1968), pp. 246–248.

> Bind me ye *Woodbines* in your 'twines,
> Curle me about ye gadding *Vines*,
> And Oh so close your Circles lace,
> That I may never leave this Place;
> But, lest your Fetters prove too weak,
> Ere I your Silken Bondage break,
> Do you, *O Brambles*, chain me too,
> And courteous *Briars* nail me through.
>
> [609–616]

Then, abruptly and mysteriously, the meadows are restored to order, as if enacting that renovation of all the creatures made possible by that other crucifixion. The meadows are yet more fresh and green; the river, regaining its banks, orders and unifies the meadows by reflecting all things within itself as in a crystal mirror. But the speaker is still utterly passive; he blends himself into the newly restored harmony as a compleat angler lazily fishing on the river banks in a condition of contented irresponsibility. It is upon this scene that Maria Fairfax appears.

Maria is the true descendant of Donne's Elizabeth Drury. *Pace* Don Cameron Allen and Frank Manley, I do not see her as an Athena or Sophia figure, a symbol of Heavenly Wisdom, but as the twelve-year-old daughter of "Fairfax and the starry Vere," the pupil of Marvell who had a gift for languages and excellent marriage prospects. She is the culminating principle of order in the poem, and the appropriate force to resolve its issues, in that she recapitulates—as innocent young maiden, as regenerate Christian soul, as image of God restored—something of that power which man in his pristine innocence had to enhance the order of nature:

> Tis *She* that to these Gardens gave
> That wondrous Beauty which they have;
> *She* straightness on the Woods bestows;
> To *Her* the Meadow sweetness owes;
> Nothing could make the River be
> So Chrystal-pure but only *She*;
> *She* yet more Pure, Sweet, Streight, and Fair,
> Then Gardens, Woods, Meads, Rivers are.
>
> Therefore what first *She* on them spent,
> They gratefully again present.
>
> [689–698]

Accordingly, as she walks forth "loose" nature, responding to that ordering principle in man restored by grace, "recollects" itself from its disposition to carelessness or disorder and takes on its highest perfection: the sun goes more carefully to bed, the halcyon comes forth, the air and stream and fishes are "vitrified" by her presence—in some ways recalling nature's response to the event of Christ's Incarnation as described in Milton's hymn *On the Morning of Christ's Nativity*. Maria's power to evoke this response is specifically attributed to "her *Flames*, in *Heaven* try'd" (l. 687). The amazing forcefulness of the imagery describing her walk—she is as a "new-born *Comet*" drawing a train through the sky; she "rushes" through the evening—makes a striking counterpoise to the speaker's passivity. Maria not only accepts the human responsibility to enhance the order of nature, but also to order corrupt society, and in this sphere she deals effectively with all those wanton suitors whose "artillery" of profane love is trained against her. In this she is an antitype of the Virgin Thwaites, for she is not seduced as that Eve-figure was by false or perverted views of nature and religion; rather, echoing the creative and restorative role of Mary the Virgin-Mother, Maria awaits the natural unfolding of her marital "Destiny" so that she may entail the estate in a continuing line of goodness. At the end of the poem the contrast is sharply drawn between the chaotic macrocosm of the world in the disordered condition the Fall has brought it to—"a rude heap together hurl'd / All negligently overthrown" and the "Map" or sketch of paradise which, by reason of the ordering principle in regenerate man, the Fairfax estate is. It is *"Heaven's Center, Nature's Lap. / And Paradice's only Map."*

The speaker's progress through the estate is brought to an end by Maria's departure and the coming of evening. As the salmon fishers prepare to go home, their boats on their heads like shoes, we are invited to recall the Antipodes where conditions are the flat reverse of those we know, the paradoxical state of men as "rational Amphibii," and the existence of the "dark Hemisphere" which slowly encroaches upon and (temporarily but regularly) blots out from sight the harmony of man and nature which we have seen. It is a reminder, conveyed wittily and with Marvell's vast awareness of paradox and ambiguity, of how tenuously held are all visions of human order, even that embodied in the Fairfax estate and epitomized in Maria.

IV

I have been arguing that Herbert's *The Temple* and Vaughan's *Silex Scintillans* are alike informed by a pervasive and essentially Protestant use of typology, which contributes centrally to their realization as coherent bodies of religious poetry of great imaginative power and impressive artistry. For Herbert, the most remarkable features are: the translation of the biblical types into their antitypical fulfillments in the heart of the particular speaker; the conception of the Book of Psalms as model for a collection of Christian lyrics; and the unification of the entire volume in terms of a highly individual adaptation of the Temple / Church typology. For Vaughan, who carries further certain Protestant tendencies in exegesis, the typological mode helps to define and explore the controlling metaphor of the speaker as Christian pilgrim, often simply recapitulating rather than fulfilling certain Old Testament types of that pilgrimage. Also, remarkably, Vaughan portrays the speaker's spiritual experience as a concrete historical embodiment of the paradigms for the spiritual life defined by the Protestant allegorical reading of the Song of Solomon. What results is a fusion of the allegorical and the typological modes, in which the allegorical is probably primary. Marvell's *Upon Appleton House* adapts typological symbolism to the presentation of metaphysically based secular praises and allusions to public events. The secular, public context promotes in this poem a thoroughgoing development of the Protestant conception of history as a continuum, as well as a forthright alteration of the terms of the typological equation from type and antitype to biblical paradigm and its recapitulations in the course of providential history. Significantly enough, for all three works the typological mode provides in very different ways a unifying symbolic perspective which orders without at all reducing their rich multiplicity and complexity.

IV

A LITTLE LOOK INTO CHAOS

Robert M. Adams

This is a topic without a bibliography and a paper almost without footnotes. I say this not out of bravado, but mournfully. It would have been nice to find other people's definitions, descriptions, and doctrines of Milton's Chaos, for guidance and support, as well as the always welcome occasions of polemic. But I was unable to find more than passing remarks on the subject, and will welcome suggestions as to where else I should look. And it would have been nice to get in a reference or two to my favorite Miltonic source, Rupertus Tuitensis or some other suitably occult figure. But my interest is not in where Milton got his Chaos but in what he did when he got it. So this rather limits the erudition one can display without making ostentation an end in itself. Hence the poor, sparse, speculative paper which follows—a paper over which I would like to inscribe a spectacular and gigantic question mark, emblematic of all the open questions I feel clustering around the paper. Can the poem usefully be seen from such a special angle? Why hasn't anybody ever tried it before? What authority can an "outside" interpretation like this have against the Christian humanist morality that has held the strong right-center position in Miltonic criticism for so long against so many antagonists? It would be nice if these questions could be asked from some safe, neutral position—noncommitally, as it were. But as we don't know what a question can do till we put some heart and energy into asking it, I've chosen to take my chances.

In talking about Chaos in Milton's great poem, it's probably prudent to start by locating it along a couple of different coordinates, by trying to say what it is and where it is and when it is, in the cosmos that Milton imagined as well as in the poem he wrote. A lot of this preliminary material will be familiar, and for that I apologize; but it's a topic that's generally peripheral to the focus of our interests as we read *Paradise Lost*; and a quick reminder of the circumstances may get our collective feet under us.

Chaos, then, is situated in one of Milton's universes—in the big universe, with Heaven at the top, Hell at the bottom, and no other determinate shape at all—Chaos occupies in this universe a middle position. Heaven is on top, as presumably it always was; Hell is on the bottom. Since it was prepared for the fallen angels—

> Such place eternal justice had prepared
> For those rebellious, here their prison ordained
> In utter darkness—
>
> [I, 70–72]

Hell can hardly have been in existence before there were any rebels. That would involve attributing to God almost too much foresight, and too malicious a character. Yet Milton does specify "eternal justice," and this reminds us that God rules the whole cosmos, from top to bottom, from beginning to end. (It may help with the passage if we read the word "utter" as "complete," not as "outer," since Hell is in no sense outside God's providence.) If He did not create Hell for the bad angels before they fell, to be ready for them when they did fall, He certainly foresaw the necessity of doing so. Hell therefore is a subtraction from Chaos, which previously had no lower boundary at all. Speaking to Satan, the Anarch himself complains that his kingdom has been diminished by two recent subtractions:

> first Hell
> Your dungeon stretching far and wide beneath;
> Now lately Heaven and Earth, another World
> Hung o'er my realm.
>
> [II, 1002–1005]

We notice, in passing, that "Heaven" has been newly created too, as Chaos sees the matter—"Heaven and Earth." He is not only echoing Genesis 1, but distinguishing the nine empyreal spheres of the created cosmos from the eternal heaven of God's presence.

So Chaos is a large, elastic, disorderly place between two fixed and essentially unchanging planes of existence. Hell is immutably and unremittingly evil; it is dark and low, as dark as you can get ("utter darkness") and as low as you can go. When Satan in his soliloquy atop Niphates contemplates a deeper hell than that in which he now suffers, it isn't physical depth (because I think there isn't anything lower than the fiery soil on which Pandemonium stands), it's psychological depth of suffering that he envisages:

> Which way I fly is hell, myself am hell;
> And in the lowest deep a lower deep
> Still threatening to devour me opens wide,
> To which the hell I suffer seems a heaven.
>
> [IV, 75–78]

Heaven is immutably and eternally good; it is bright and high. Chaos is the area of change and struggle in between. The created cosmos (heaven and earth together) is actually hung in the midst of Chaos; God created it out of Chaos, and at the end of recorded history it will revert to Chaos, when heaven and hell are closed up, the world consumed with fire, and nature comes to an end. Chaos, Milton tells us in a tremendous line, is

> The womb of nature and perhaps her grave.[1]

That is, to explicate what is perhaps already clear enough, Chaos contained from the beginning the seeds of those elements (earth, air, water, fire) of which the natural world was created by the imposition of divine order, and to which it will ultimately revert. Chaos is the baseline or norm from which the special purposes of God raised the cosmos, and to which (so far as the special purposes of God will allow) the cosmos will automatically relapse after the Last Judgment. Let us note that Chaos, though spatially at the center of Milton's largest universe (between the limiting

---

[1] It is customary to cite as the classical analogue for this line Lucretius, V, 260: "Omniparens, eadem rerum commune sepulchrum."

districts of Heaven and Hell), is temporally at the outer limits. It bounds the temporal extent of the cosmos, and for that matter of the poem. We cannot see beyond it, either before or after. "Beyond is all abyss," says Adam (XII, 555); the word is constantly associated with Chaos (as in II, 917, 969, 1027 and VII, 211, 234); and indeed if we add darkness to disorder, there is no need to look or imagine further. "Et sine fine Chaos, & sine fine Deus," says S. B., M. D., in one of the two poems dedicatory to *Paradise Lost,* the second edition. In time, if not in space, the two powers are coextensive.

Whether Chaos provided the original raw material for God's Heaven (in the precreation dimension) we do not know and are not encouraged to guess; but, Heaven apart, it is quite explicit that everything else in the cosmos is disguised (i.e., organized) Chaos, which could be jolted back, with relative ease, into Chaos again. Milton steers clear of specifying Chaos overtly as a possible outcome of the war in heaven, but he hints at it:

> and now all heaven
> Had gone to wrack, with ruin overspread,
> Had not th'Almighty Father, etc.
>
> [VI, 669–71]

The bridge that Sin and Death build over Chaos seems to be another encroachment on the Anarch's kingdom, and as Satan passes down the bridge, Chaos snarls resentfully at him:

> on either side
> Disparted Chaos over-built exclaimed,
> And with rebounding surge the bars assailed
> That scorned his indignation.
>
> [X, 415–18]

But in bringing Sin and Death to the world, the bridge fulfills almost to the word the last prophetic words of Chaos to Satan:

> Havoc and spoil and ruin are my gain.
>
> [II, 1009]

It has long been remarked that Satan, in reporting back to the cohorts awaiting him in Pandemonium, exaggerates the obstacles he had faced, and exaggerates by implication his own accomplishments, in saying that "Chaos wild / . . . fiercely opposed /

My journey strange" (X, 477–79). In fact Chaos in his own person actually helped Satan along. The point may be scored off against Satan (he is a *miles gloriosus*), or else it is a way of softening the evident circumstance that in the warfare between God and Satan, though neither participant wants this outcome, Chaos is the one immediate and obvious gainer. Satan's victory on earth has not been a thwarting of Chaos, but an expansion of his ancient empire. Chaos, out of which the Ptolemaic "heaven and earth" were created no longer ago than Book VII, and which has bounded and surrounded that Ptolemaic cosmos ever since, has largely reestablished itself already in Book X—as if to provide a paradigm of the way in which the larger universe also will pass, over a somewhat longer period of time, from Chaos to Chaos, with a little period of partial order in between.

Chaos as ancient Emperor of a nonempire, anarch not monarch, is a figure of grim Miltonic paradox, strong only in his weakness. All other empires grow by extending their controls and powers, his only by letting go. He is not even positive enough to claim empire for himself, for it is the standard of his consort Night that he proposes to advance—Night, "eldest of things" (II, 962), "unoriginal Night" (X, 477). The epithets strongly reemphasize that Night in this poem is not daughter of Chaos (as she is in Hesiod, who tells us directly, "From Chaos came forth Erebus and black Night," verse 123); if anything, the parental relation runs the other way. If Night were the mother of Chaos, as well as his consort, she would parallel Sin in her relation to Death and emphasize darkness as the ultimate enemy of divine light; but Chaos himself, containing seeds of light as well as darkness, is interestingly ambivalent in his relation to the warfare between the poem's more "positive" powers.

More positive powers? Curiously, when we look at Chaos for a while, we start to see some surprisingly positive aspects of Satan—he looks more like an opponent, a dramatic antagonist, even a foil, than like an enemy. But before we start pursuing this tantalizing rabbit, let's dispose of the last of our preliminaries by noting that the composition of Milton's poem *does* make it necessary for us to look at Chaos, or think of Chaos, again and again. In this respect, Milton's poem is quite unlike those of his two classical predecessors in chaotic description, Hesiod and Ovid. Both use Chaos as a kind of starting point in their poems, depart from it, and never come back. But Milton's poem, whether by accident or design (and with Milton that's never a real option) returns to Chaos over and over. There is of course the great panorama of Book II, when Satan is about to venture forth, followed by the encounter in the pavilion; there is an equivalent description, involving some parallels, in Book VII, when God ventures into Chaos in order to create the Ptolemaic universe. Sin and Death venture into it very graphically in Book X, the angels fall through it, hurtling out of control in Books I and VI. Literally described, it recurs again and again—of the first ten books only IV and IX fail to mention it specifically. And by implication, innuendo, recall, metaphor—that is quite a long story, to which we shall come later.

Chaos is present or potentially present throughout Milton's poem, and it represents a very deeply felt image of evil as essential weakness. Saint Augustine tells us somewhere that the devil himself is an advocate of peace; he must have certain varieties and areas and levels of peace, in order to be more effectually malicious. But Chaos is neutral as between good and evil; all he likes is disorder. That inclines him to evil, of course, but not all the way, for evil is itself a principle of order; and Chaos, is, so to speak, beyond good and evil. I do not think anyone before Milton represented Chaos as he did, under the guise of a feeble, tongue-tied old monarch unable to command even his own features. "With faltering speech and visage uncomposed"—it is an image of utter breakdown and loss of control. For a poet whose epic aspirations call for him to make his way across vast physical and imaginative distances, to organize immense bodies of material, to poise a fictive world in the void, the figure of Chaos could represent an authentic psychic menace.

But I want to consider in the poem the two positive forces who are common enemies of Chaos, and whose hostility to each other has been so lavishly emphasized, has absorbed so much partisan energy, that even to talk of their cooperation smacks of paradox. Satan is, I propose, in service to God in a variety of ways that mostly involve their common enmity to Chaos. A first and very simple way of seeing this is in the matter of space. I hope it's not too obvious to say that Satan by establishing his headquarters in Hell—Down There—creates a range of physical and moral possibility for man; he structures the cosmos. A universe consisting of just two parts, Heaven and Chaos, is essentially undirected and incomprehensible. In Heaven, a state of absolute bliss and perfect fulfillment, one feels no deficiency, hence no desire or purpose. In Chaos, one is out of touch with everything; one can't

see or conceive or desire (with a fixed purpose) Heaven or anything else. One can't fear a fall because there is no down to fall
to. It is a place, or rather than a place, a condition.

> Without dimension, where length, breadth, and height
> And time and place are lost.
>
> [II, 893–94]

If it weren't for Hell, Chaos would be bound to imply a state of
weightlessness, as there would be nothing below to exert gravi-
tational force. Satan, by falling, gives the cosmos a bottom and a
sense of moral and physical distance. By not only giving the
cosmos an up and down (one inconceivable without the other),
but by tying that up and down to a moral dimension, Satan gives
the universe a shape. Simply by falling, he measures distance and
points a direction; he is God's first plumb-bob. And by tying
morality in with our sense of vertical direction, he triggers an
automatic, an instinctive reaction. Fear of falling is, we are told,
one of man's first and deepest instincts.[2] Adam doesn't fall phys-
ically at all. It's obvious that his fall is a very serious act, but
equally obvious that it doesn't take such a deep and terrifying
form as Satan's. Satan falls in terror, out of control, Adam at
most in dismay. To make another comparison (for my intent is
simply to show how much Satan's physical fall into Hell adds to
the emotional tone of the poem), only compare the depth and
complexity of our feeling about Hell with our feelings about
Heaven in the poem. We know vividly how one gets into Hell—
by falling violently and helplessly for nine days and nights.
How to get into Heaven is a much more mysterious, much less
definite process. For one thing, we never see anyone do it; we
see them only after they are already there, and what they experience we are forced to imagine for ourselves. Satan adds a physical dimension to Milton's moral universe, making up be really
up, down be absolutely way far down, and good be all the better
because it is diametrically *not* evil. He knots our moral feelings
tightly to our basic physical instincts—serving in all this didactic
ends which are both Miltonic and (so to speak) divine.

Satan not only structures the world spatially, he does so tem-

---

[2] We note in the matter of Satan the serpent, vulture, and toad how concerned Milton is to connect his devil with creatures from which we feel instinctive revulsion. Our love for God and attraction to Him are based on high,
"spiritual" principles—a large perspective, an enlightened point of view, logic,
gratitude. Our responses to evil are intuitional.

porally; at the very moment when he seems to be defying God most vigorously, he serves God's ends, and the ends of the poem, by an act of definition in time. The question concerns simply the point of Satan's own origin. It is not easy to work out, from the several assertions and counterassertions of the poem, what precisely constituted Milton's "doctrine" in this matter, if he had one. In a passage of his first soliloquy atop Mount Niphates, Satan speaks remorsefully of his own ingratitude toward God:

>   he deserv'd no such return
> From me, whom he created what I was
> In that bright eminence.
>
>   [IV, 42–44]

But in public debate with Abdiel before the masses of revolted angels, Satan has quite another story:

> We know no time when we were not as now;
> Know none before us, self-begot, self-raised
> By our quickening power, when fatal course
> Had circled his full orb, the birth mature
> Of this our native heaven, ethereal sons.
>
>   [V, 859–63]

Commentary has traditionally contrasted these private and public postures of Satan in order to emphasize the sinful arrogance of the latter. In declaring his independence of his Maker, Satan is said to be guilty of a kind of hubris for which, to the reader's edification, he will shortly be punished. And the conscientious annotator sends us off to rummage through the *Christian Doctrine* in search of that passage (it is I, vii) where Milton, on the very shaky authority of Numbers 16:22 and 27:16, declares roundly that the angels were created "at some particular period."

So this is evidently Milton's "doctrine," delivered in his own literal person; and Satan, in claiming to be independent of God, is a bad fellow, a boaster, and a hypocrite. He denies his Maker in a way that we would be most ill-advised to imitate. Morally, I daresay this is right; from a narrative point of view, Milton may even have wanted to score the point against Satan. But in terms of the Miltonic "argument" ("to justify the ways of God to men"), the more vigorously Satan asserts his independence, especially in the act of revolt, the better he serves his function in the economy of the poem and the economy of God's cosmos. That function is to remove from God responsibility for the evil in the world by assuming that responsibility himself. Only suppose that, in the act of revolt, Satan were to pursue that line of thought which he began in the soliloquy atop Niphates: "God created me what I was—bright, eminent, and doomed to fall. I am his creature; he made me: at any moment he can destroy me; whatever I do, I do, not only by his permission but with powers of his granting, the full consequences of which he foreknew at the time of my creation. I am not only his creature, but his agent." A creaturely devil, delivering himself of mealy-mouthed sentiments like that, and shifting the blame for the imperfect cosmos onto his Maker, would be worse, from Milton's point of view, than no devil at all. For one of Satan's major functions in the poem is to *stop* that line of questioning which leads back ineluctably from the present evil, whatever it may be—back from ancestor to ancestor, from wrong to wrong, back down the trail of history, all the way to Adam, who blamed Eve, who blamed the serpent, who would have blamed Satan had he been able to speak. And if Satan will not stop the line of blame there, what is to prevent it from going back all the way to the maker of all things, to God himself? Satan has to be an opaque, self-generated, self-sustained figure, at least in his own conceit. He has to be a figure without the dimension of inner questioning that would lead him into the pit of his own motivation—a figure who absorbs our questions and stops them through a kind of inner blindness—who is given so much momentum to begin with that the reader never pauses to ask what is the source of his first energy. By being such a figure, Satan becomes the chief bulwark of God, a lightning rod for his protection from the only enemy he has to fear in the poem, a resentful human conscience. "Who's to blame for this awful mess in which we see the world?" A great deal that has been dismissed as "sinful" in Satan's character serves in fact to fit him for an important and difficult role in relation to this question: he is a scapegoat. Symbolically, we hate the scapegoat. We load on him all the sins of the tribe, and to demonstrate our aversion, we drive him out into the wilderness, we separate ourselves from him in every way possible. But there is another inevitable component in our feelings about him; it is not admiration or hero worship by any means; it is relief, it is gratitude. He carries off an element of ourselves

that we want to purge, to excrete, to dispose of.[3] Without trying to define at all precisely what is very difficult to put into
words, we may speak sketchily of the static electricity of life
that we must, so to speak, "ground" somewhere. Satan is a
ground for these feelings in us, as well as for a good deal else
in the poem—including our resentful sense that someone besides
ourselves must be "to blame" for the way things are.

Satan is probably a very bad fellow to deny that he is the son
of God, but he is also a very good fellow for the same reason.
And it must be added that neither God nor Milton nor anybody
else in the poem insists very warmly that Satan *is* the creation
of God—if indeed he is. Repeated description of the Son as
"only begotten Son" effectually keeps one from feeling that any
of the angels, good or bad, are properly children of God the
Father. Created they may have been, begotten they were not:
we are left to imagine, as idle speculation moves us, what curious
process of fabrication brought them all into being, with their
differing potentialities for good and evil.

In taking responsibility for the sum of evil in the world—taking it boldly, without seeming to be aware of the tremendous
sacrifice he is making—Satan grounds the reverse lightning of
blame. In passing, he removes much of the load of guilt from the
two human actors. From the point of view of Adam and Eve,
the Fall is an episode that was all over before either of them
knew it had happened; from Satan's point of view, the scene in
the garden is the climax of a long-laid plot, which we have seen
devised and proposed and carried out, in spite of enormous difficulties, with malicious evil as its deliberate end. So, inevitably,
we attribute to Satan most of the blame for the Fall; not only so,
man by departing from the Satanic example of reaction after the
fall can limit rather easily the consequences of his own disaster.
In other words, Satan, by taking the heavy rap, shows the seri-
ousness of the crime; man, by appealing to the clemency of the
judge, shows the basic benevolence of the establishment. It is
relatively easy to obtain mercy when someone else has provoked
and established the rigorous process of justice.

I have been thus large in setting forth the mock contest or col-
lusion (game?) between God and Satan as it might appear from
the viewpoint of the old Anarch, Chaos, in order to suggest how
warily Milton must have proceeded with his two great contest-

[3] Cf. Denis Saurat, *Milton, Man and Thinker* (New York, 1925), p. 220:
"Milton had Satan in him and wanted to drive him out."

ants lest the only victor be too patently the third empire of weakness and contradiction. The imperial parallel between God and Satan is reinforced throughout the poem: they are rival emperors, sitting on "equal" and opposite thrones, ruling by means of a close council through a general assembly; they hold consults, issue edicts, man the battlements, review the troops, decide on imperial policies. A persistent strain of imagery identifies Satan with the Turkish Sophi; the empire of Heaven is just as distinctly based on Revelations and Ezekiel. But they are both organized empires; and, as with most imperial conflicts, theirs are full of absurdity. Neither participant wishes to abolish the other, or can even envisage such an outcome, since that would involve assuming full responsibility for the governance of things. God wants Satan to be responsible for the wrong and evil in the world, and Satan, with surprisingly little resistance, accepts the responsibility. The result of their mingled intentions and self-restrictions, is a partial, muted, and metaphorical reassertion of the sway of Chaos in the last books of the poem. With prophetic insight, no less a personage than Mammon had suggested something like such an outcome during the Great Consult:

> him to unthrone we then
> May hope when everlasting fate shall yield
> To fickle chance, and chaos judge the strife.
>
> [II, 231–33]

God is not unthroned, of course, nor does everlasting fate yield unconditionally to fickle chance. But God's providence is in some major way withdrawn from our little world as a result of the fall; disorder and chance take the place of design in the shape of it; and as the focus of the poem narrows and lengthens to fit the dimensions of human history, the war of the two empires (which had organized the cosmos, divided it, and arranged it) disappears in the distance. Man's fate is now to struggle with that limited Chaos which the indecisive and apparently indefinite conflict of God and Satan has allowed to seep back into the immediate affairs of men. Chaos in this last part of the epic is nowhere named, nor specifically described; it has become part of the air we breathe. Its presence is felt in three contexts particularly: in the exterior structure of the world, in the history of man, and in his most inward workings, his psyche.

A notable instance of Chaos asserting itself in the external cos-

mos occurs when the angels, at God's behest (but that behest
was itself dictated by Satan's successful seduction of man), disorder the structure of the solar system so as to allow the planets
to shed now benign and now malignant influence on man and
his earth. It's reasonably clear that Milton felt that astrology was
a mathematical science, enabling men to predict if not to control the influence of the planets. Raphael had rebuked Adam's
vain and fruitless curiosity about the working of the stars and so
he might when their influence was unfailingly benign; but after
the fall, a knowledge of astrology is apparently going to be crucial to the prudent conduct of human life. More striking even
than this change, is the action of the angels in modifying the
earth's weather:

> to the winds they set
> Their corners, when with bluster to confound
> Sea, air, and shore, the thunder when to roll
> With terror through the dark aerial hall.
>
> [X, 664–67]

This is surely to bring back some element of that Chaos which
consisted

> Of neither sea, nor shore, nor air, nor fire
> But all these in their pregnant causes mixed
> Confusedly, and which thus must ever fight.
>
> [II, 912–14]

It is the same thing, the mixing of the elements; yet Milton has
taken a little edge off the parallel by almost leaving out the
fourth element of fire. *Almost* I say, because it's there by implication in connection with the thunder roll. Earth, air, and water
are confounded by the winds, with fire flashing just offstage;
and this is Chaos itself. We recall, in this matter of winds, how
much of Satan's journey through Chaos consisted of a struggle
through conflicting winds, how often we hear of the

> ever-threatening storms
> Of Chaos blustering round, inclement sky.
>
> [III, 425–26]

When we were first introduced to Chaos, there was a proviso
that the fight of elements must continue forever,

Unless th'Almighty maker them ordain
His dark materials to create more worlds.

[II, 915–16]

But in Book X the unleashing of the winds to confound the elements is a way of surrendering to chaos part of an already-
created world.

I don't suppose I have to labor the various ways in which
Chaos is involved in stories like those of the Flood and the
Tower of Babel; what's strikingly different in them is that the
architect of confusion is the Lord himself. Doubtless he is justified many times over in punishing the wickedness of man; yet
this puts him in the middle of the chain of blame, doing one
evil because of another, and out of this logic only Chaos can
profit. The curse of Babel is an impressive instance of a major
human disorder, the immediate source of which is God's deliberate decree. Instead of Satan taking the blame and saving God
from it, God must stand in the foreground and save Satan, in
the remote background, from blame. There couldn't be a clearer
instance of how Chaos seeps into the postlapsarian Miltonic
world, despite the intentions of either the forces of good or the
forces of evil. And as we look at the recurrent action of human
history in the last books of *Paradise Lost,* we see it to be a constant slumping into weakness and confusion. Satan doesn't directly contribute to this falling off, Chaos is never mentioned;
but the utmost heroism is demanded, again and again, of some
isolated Christian hero who is called on to redeem the time from
its inherent tendency to corruption. Such an impersonal phenom-
enon as the tangle of diseases with which Adam is confronted in
Book XI is not the work of a single personal agent; all the ail-
ments are comprehensible as a single condition, intemperance,
which is disorder and disproportion in the economy of the body.
Man himself has created them, man in the corrupted state for
which Satan is, doubtless, ultimately responsible. But no specific
force in the macrocosmos is made directly responsible for man's
catastrophic state. It is the new constitution of things, or the old
constitution just allowed to reassert itself (Satan was sick before
man was created). In withdrawing the picket line of angels
around the Garden, and letting Adam and Eve wander forth into
the gross, impure air of a lower world, does God create a new
balance of forces or simply free and old one to assert itself? Milton does not say with any decisiveness. Our feeling, as readers

with a human, not an angelic perspective, can only be that the withdrawal of heavenly protection (against disease and bad weather, for example) is the termination of a special exemption, and the resumption of an ordinary condition, within which Chaos has a certain matter-of-course role to play. No plots or apparatus are required; when the deliberately interposed shield is lifted, things crumble of their own "natural impulse." Adam's agonized cry—

> Both Death and I
> Am found Eternal, and incorporate both—

sounds at the depth of his remorseful monologue (X, 815–16). He could just as well cry that Chaos and he are now incorporate, except that death is the special exquisite privilege of the animate world—Chaos is less fiercely felt because it is now incorporate with the inanimate as well as the animate world. It has become mingled with the substance of things—homogenized chaos.

Finally, in the realm of psychology, the Fall has long been understood as an explicit reversal of ideal order, an upheaval and invasion of emotional, irrational chaos into the ordered processes of Adam and Eve as they were created. When our great parents fall first to lust and then to quarreling, once more it's conflicting winds that image forth their inner chaos:

> Nor only tears
> Rained at their eyes, but high winds worse within
> Began to rise, high passions—anger, hate,
> Mistrust, suspicion, discord—and shook sore
> Their inward state of mind, calm region once
> And full of peace, now tost and turbulent.
>
> [IX, 1121–26]

The parallel with other blustering and turbulent winds is too obvious and deliberate to need enforcing; at the root of it is, of course, the old physiology of the humors, according to which moods and emotional states were the consequence of interior winds, ill-compounded and ill-managed. Beyond this immediate occasion, moreover, we can hardly help noticing, over the last two books of the poem, a curious and surely deliberate excess in Adam's emotional responses to the historical events he is shown or told about. He is delighted with the idyllic existence of the Sethites—Milton excuses him as "soon inclined to admit delight, / The bent of nature" (XI, 596–97)—and has to be warned against judging by the mere appearance of things. He is in abject despair at the vision of the Flood, and has to be encouraged to see the brighter side of things. In dramatic terms, this is perfectly understandable. Starting from a state of almost perfect innocence, Adam is required to understand and assume the weight of all human history, and given very little time in which to do it. The purpose of his education is precisely to give him some perspective on things—to temper him toward a nice blend of assurance and humility. By erring, first in the direction of complacency, then in the direction of despair, he works his way toward a difficult emotional balance. His conscience, he learns, must be a vigilant and scrupulous warrior against the world's continual forays on his peace of mind. After the angelic guard around Paradise strikes camp, only the sentinel conscience remains on lonely guard. And the evil against which it remains alert is no longer a big dark flying man in a suit of armor—it is built into the very structure of the cosmos, of society, of the mind within which conscience itself patrols. It is not an empire, to be fought by ranked battalions; it is discord, passivity, weakness—Chaos, in other words, seen not from the outside as a stuttering, moping old man with a facial tic, but from the inside, as a constant ingredient of the Christian life, an intimate, and ultimately invincible enemy.

Reactions to a scholarly paper generally involve two traditional elements in uneasy combination:

(1) it's a pack of nonsense, and
(2) we knew it all the time.

Looking back over what I've said so far, I'm inclined to agree with both these comments, and to see in the making of them the salvation of my argument. If I have any insight to bring to the reading of *Paradise Lost*, it derives from applying both these useful cliches at once to the discussion I've laid out so far.

My paper about Chaos is essentially a pack of nonsense because it goes pervasively against the grain and structure of *Paradise Lost* itself, making primary and consecutive what Milton, for excellent reasons of his own, left intermittent and peripheral. I sin here in pretty good company, but I sin nonetheless. A skeptic could shrink the matter over which I've made such ado to

small proportions indeed. Milton, he would say, had certain in-
escapable geographical facts to cope with: Hell, Earth, and
Heaven are bound to lie at some distance from one another, and
to have some minimal, representable stuff in between; Creation,
to be shown in a poem, has to be creation from some basic substance. Chaos was simply Milton's way of killing these two birds
with one stone. Having it already there, he used it wherever else
he needed it in the poem; but he gave it no universal allegorical
significance, and there's no particular reason to think Milton
meant Chaos to be felt in the last two books, silently encroaching
on those three fields of existence. If he had any such intentions,
he might well have mentioned Chaos or used the adjective "chaotic"—in other words, made explicit what he deliberately left
unexpressed. Writing a paper about "Chaos" in *Paradise Lost*
is almost as mechanical, as computerly a process, as writing
a paper about Milton's use of the color green, the quality of
hardness, or triangular shapes. All you need to write this sort
of paper is monomania.

So far with the first objector. The second one is also right.
Nobody reads *Paradise Lost* without feeling the power and
terror of the Chaos whom Satan encounters out there in inter-
galactic space; and no half-wakeful reader has failed to see that
Chaos, as a concept if not a figure, continues to exert pressure
on the latter part of the poem. How far precisely that pressure
extends may be questioned; but we've all felt it, as what Milton
plainly intended, a marginal element. You, therefore, who have
always treated it as a marginal element, are in a better position
to assess its importance than is someone who focuses on it, and
strains to see it wherever there's the least hint of its potential
existence. The man who sees the nuances of a text in their
proper light can never be a man who's concentrating on nuances.

I'm not unaware that there are ways to turn these methodological arguments around, upside down, and insight out; for
the moment, what we open up here is a problematic which focuses on a relatively simple question: for the purposes of the
poem, how much weight should we allow to the figure of Chaos
and the perspectives which an awareness of his presence unfolds?
I'm happy to concede that in this paper, I've overstated the case
for his presence, and traced out the implications of his logic as
vigorously as I could—too vigorously for the good of the poem.
We must suppress Chaos a little bit, mute him, sit (maybe) on

his head, so that the poem as a whole may maintain its intended balance. On the other hand, it may help to be made aware of his unsettling presence, if only to appreciate better Milton's art in managing the other energies of his fable. Chaos is an operative element in the balance if only by being himself so radically unstable an element.

There are reasons, thus, to push Chaos forward in the poem, and reasons to push him back; to which I would add, as a fundamental consideration, that he may serve to recall a special quality of Milton's mind—its ability to pursue its moral ends across several complex mythic structures and metaphors in close succession. There's a way of saying this that makes it sound like an accusation of mental confusion. I mean no such thing. I mean only that none of the many metaphors Milton used expressed his moral insight as largely as Dante's central spatial metaphors expressed *his* moral insight. Warfare, for example, expresses part, but only part, of Milton's vision of how a saint serves God in this world. Abstention from temptation is another form of service; so is delight in the natural richness of the world and gratitude for its beauty. Life is a quest, a race, a battle; it is service to cause, pursuit of a pattern. No image is more deeply rooted in Milton's mind as a metaphor of spiritual insight, than the image of light. The radiance of God's grace illumines man's darkened mind; through the Gospels and the Book of Creatures alike, his light pours upon us. Our role is to clear our eyes, open our hearts, purify our senses, and accept the divine infusions as sincerely as we can. A mighty nation cannot have too much light; and in a famous passage, Milton compares England to "an Eagle muing her mighty youth, and kindling her undazl'd eyes at the full midday beam; purging and unscaling her long-abused sight at the fountain itself of heav'nly radiance." Yet at the same time, and in the same splendid piece of prose, there is another metaphor for truth, one that implies very different attitudes toward it, and very different behavior in its regard. The myth that Milton adopts momentarily, with no apparent sense of its incongruity with that which he uses so liberally elsewhere, is a deeply "chaotic" fable; it assumes the presence of chaos and disorder at the very heart of religious light—the near-indistinguishability of saving truth and grievous error:

Truth indeed came once into the world with her divine Master, and was a perfect shape most glorious to look on: but when he ascended, and his Apostles after him were laid asleep, then strait arose a wicked race of deceivers, who as that story goes of the *Aegyptian Typhon* with his conspirators, how they dealt with the good *Osiris*, took the virgin Truth, hewd her lovely form into a thousand pieces, and scatter'd them to the four winds. From that time ever since, the sad friends of Truth, such as durst appear, imitating the careful search that *Isis* made for the mangl'd body of *Osiris*, went up and down gathering up limb by limb still as they could find them. We have not found them all, Lords and Commons, nor ever shall doe till her Masters second comming: he shall bring together every joynt and member, and shall mould them into an immortall feature of loveliness and perfection. Suffer not these licensing prohibitions to stand at every place of opportunity, forbidding and disturbing them that continue seeking, that continue to do our obsequies to the torn body of our martyr'd Saint.[4]

If we let the second myth carry over into the first, it would seem to say that we must painfully assemble the sun before we can rise like an eagle to stare undazzled at the full midday beam. If we let the first myth carry over into the second, it minimizes the difficulty of assembling the god, because every piece would be as radiant as the sun itself—would carry its own instant hallmark of bright divinity. Each of the myths is true to a fragment of Milton's experience, Milton's intent. It seems idle to try to legislate here. Milton has left us an open space, for which, as readers, we should be duly grateful; it is an area where we can adjust values and assign relative weights to the elements of his thought, as seems most convenient to ours. If our reading of *Paradise Lost* strikes a poised and natural balance without any necessity of bringing Chaos explicitly into the account, well, so much the better. But if we find William Empson and A. J. A. Waldock at frantic odds with T. S. Eliot and C. S. Lewis, the moral readings of the poem being used to dull the aesthetic highlights, and discussion of the great poem deteriorating here and there toward a slanging match between God's Own Boys and the Devil's Disciples, then a little look into Chaos may serve a reconciling purpose.

In this whole business we may get a momentary perspective on critical alternatives by alluding to a pair of northern California colleagues. Only one of them is a professed Miltonist, so far, but since our interest is methodology that's no great matter.

---

[4] *Areopagitica: Complete Prose Works of John Milton*, ed. Ernest Sirluck et al., Vol. II (New Haven and London), pp. 549–550, 558.

Paul Alpers repeatedly tells us, in his long and fascinating book on *The Faerie Queene* that we must "trust the verse"; Stanley Fish tells us, in an equally provocative book on *Paradise Lost*, that we mustn't on any account trust the verse—that the verse traps us into a response against the sinfulness of which Milton already has prepared a lecture. Personally, and for no better reasons perhaps than those of temperament, I'm inclined to trust the verse; and my glimpse into Chaos reinforces this instinct. It teaches me that I'm not all wrong in admiring Satan's abrupt and independent energy; it encourages me to see that in the decline of that God-Satan polarity which structures so powerfully the early books of *Paradise Lost*, Chaos presents a hidden third force leading toward The-Way-Things-Are which is more acceptable to sincere religious feeling than if either God or Satan (each qualified only by the conscious energy of the other) were allowed to control the closing energies of the poem. The Way Things Are is No Damn Good; Milton knows that, and his deftness in allowing the negative power of Chaos to assert itself, muffling and muting the active imperial rhetoric on both sides, can be appreciated as an extraordinary touch of art. There was more to his spiritual economy, I would argue, than that "egotistical sublime" which has been so generously appreciated. In this poem where history has had to be so incredibly foreshortened, there isn't really much space for the *lacrymae rerum*, but for this too Milton has found room. Chaos insinuates it; and his agency, precisely because it isn't tied to explicit benevolence or malice, makes easier that response of ours, which mingles rueful regret, reaffirmation to the "right" cause, and an awareness that nobody's intention corresponds very closely to what we have to live with.

INTERPRETATION

V

THE MUSIC OF COMUS

Louis L. Martz

The main difficulty in the criticism of *Comus* seems to lie in the multiple versions of the work.[1] There is the masque as it was first performed, for which our evidence lies in the Bridgewater manuscript and in the musical manuscripts for the five songs composed to Milton's words by Henry Lawes. There is the work as it exists, revised and unrevised, in the Trinity College manuscript, which seems to represent, in its basic version, a fair copy of some earlier manuscript—the shorter Bridgewater version being probably derived at some remove from that *ur*-manuscript. The extensive revisions in the Trinity manuscript seem to be moving toward publication, which first occurred, with important additions, in the separate printing of 1637, and then, with minor changes, in the collected volume of 1645. No one of these versions can be taken to represent the true *Comus*, for the printed version, by lacking the music, cutting some of the stage directions, and adding speeches, tends to depart from the genre that Milton announced in the only title he ever gave the work: *A Maske*. The ideal version of the work, then, exists only in the imagination, and we must strive to re-create it by fusing all these versions into one that will represent the true "music" of *Comus*.

My use of the word "music" here holds what Milton might have called a "mysterious" meaning—even a fourfold meaning.

[1] See the Bibliographical Note.

First of all, it refers to the literal sense: the actual music that we possess, in the form of the five songs by Henry Lawes. Second, it refers to additional music of this kind that may have existed, or was perhaps planned, according to various hints and directions contained in the Bridgewater manuscript, the Trinity manuscript, or the published version of the masque. Third, it refers to certain musical allusions and descriptions that exist within the poetry of the masque, often as commentary on or memory of the actual music sung. And fourth, it refers to the "music of poetry," as in Eliot's essay by that title, where Eliot refers not only to the rhythms of verse, but, in a general and metaphorical sense, to the harmony that is the entire poetical composition: "My purpose here is to insist that a 'musical poem' is a poem which has a musical pattern of sound and a musical pattern of the secondary meanings of the words which compose it, and that these two patterns are indissoluble and one." [2]

The five songs for which the music exists include (as the second, third, and fourth in the musical manuscripts) three of the verses explicitly noted as "Song" in the work itself: the Lady's Song, beginning, "Sweet Echo," the Spirit's invocation, "Sabrina Fair," and the double song of the Spirit, "Back Shepherds, back," followed by the address, "Noble Lord, and Lady Bright." The fifth song consists of the last twelve lines of the Spirit's epilogue, beginning, "Now my task is smoothly don."

The last four of these appear in the acting version, that is, in the Bridgewater manuscript, at the points where they occur in the other texts. But the first song in the musical manuscripts has a special interest, for the Bridgewater version shows that it was designed to be sung at the very beginning of the performance. For this purpose Lawes has set to music fourteen lines that, in all other versions of the masque, occur at the opening of the Spirit's epilogue. Lawes has clearly wished to open the production with song rather than with the spoken prologue in blank verse which immediately follows in the acting version. To accomplish this, the opening line of Milton's epilogue, "To the Ocean now I fly," has been changed to read: "From the Heavn's now I fly," while the rest of the song follows closely certain lines as they stand in the printed version of the Spirit's epilogue:

[2] T. S. Eliot, "The Music of Poetry," in *On Poetry and Poets* (London, 1957), p. 33.

From the Heavn's now I fly,
And those happy Climes that lie
Where day never shuts his eye,
Up in the broad Fields of the Sky,
There I suck the liquid Air
All amidst the Garden fair
Of Hesperus and his daughters three
That Sing about the golden Tree:
Iris there with humid Bow
Waters the od'rous Banks that blow
Flowers of more mingled Hew
Than her purfled scarfe can shew,
Beds of Hyacinths and Roses
Where many a Cherub soft reposes.[3]

In Milton's published epilogue, of course, the equivalent of the last line reads, "Where young *Adonis* oft reposes," and continues with the allusions to Venus, Cupid, and Psyche. There is an important advantage in opening the poem with a song, particularly with a song that includes a reference to the singing of the daughters of Hesperus; for in this way Lawes (who played the part of the Spirit, or Daemon) can prepare us to grasp the significance of musical imagery and theme throughout the masque. The Spirit is in a very important sense a presiding *musical* presence: a Neoplatonic "daemon" who helps to create a universal harmony.[4]

[3] This passage is taken from the Foss transcription of Lawes's songs as reprinted in Diekhoff, p. 243. Lineation and initial capitalization have been regularized and slight changes have been made in punctuation. With the one exception of "garden" in line 6 of the Lawes song for "gardens" (*1645*: l. 981; *Br*: l. 6), lines 2-8 of the Lawes song parallel exactly lines 977-983 of the 1645 epilogue and lines 2-8 of the Bridgewater opening. Bridgewater omits lines 984-987 in the 1645 version ("Along the crisped shades . . . all their bounties bring") and then continues in lines 9-12 with the passage "there eternall summer dwells . . . Casias balmie smells" (*1645*: ll. 988-992); the song skips this entire section and continues with "Iris there" (*Lawes*: l. 9; *1645*: l. 992; *Br*: l. 13). The next four lines (*Lawes*: ll. 9-12; *1645*: ll. 992-995; *Br*: ll. 13-16) are once again closely parallel in all three versions, as is the next-to-final line of the passage, "Beds of Hyacinths and Roses" (*Lawes*: l. 13), which reads "Hyacinth" in *1645*, Trinity, and Bridgewater. The song, however, omits the two-line section which in the other versions precedes this line; in Bridgewater and the unrevised Trinity MS this omitted section reads, "yellow, watchett, greene & blew / and drenches oft with Manna dew," while *1645* reads, "And drenches with *Elysian* dew / (List mortals, if your ears be true)." For variations in the revised Trinity MS see the Fletcher Facsimile, I, 27.

[4] Milton uses the phrase "The attendant Spirit" in the opening of the published version to refer to the figure called "A Guardian spirit or Daemon" in

In addition to these five songs, the manuscripts and the printed version of the poem contain a great deal of evidence that further music of some kind was at least planned for *Comus*. For example, Sabrina's answer, "By the rushy-fringed bank," is preceded by the direction, "Sabrina rises, attended by water-Nymphes, and sings." [5] At the same time, as Eugene Haun has noted, the last words of Sabrina's song, "I am here," form a rhyme with the Spirit's answer, "Goddess dear" (ll. 901–902). As Haun says, "To carry over the rhyme without carrying over the music would have been an error in taste which Milton with his sensitivity and Lawes with his knowledge of masque-technique would not have been likely to have committed." [6] Then thirty-five lines after this, immediately following the line, "With Groves of myrrhe and cinnamon," [7] we find in the Bridgewater and Trinity manuscripts the significant direction: "Songe ends," a direction that may be taken to imply that the intervening thirty-five lines have all been designed for music.

In a similar way, immediately after the Spirit's song of invocation, "Sabrina fair," the succeeding lines[8] are introduced in the Bridgewater manuscript with the direction: "The verse to singe or not," and then the following twenty-three lines of the poem are divided in the Bridgewater manuscript among three speakers: the elder brother, the younger brother, and the "Daemon":

> listen and appeare to vs
> in name of greate Oceanus,

Trinity and Bridgewater. As the *Variorum Commentary* points out (II, 853), "In English *daemon* had as one of its meanings . . . 'An attendant, ministering, or indwelling spirit' (*OED:* demon 1b)," but the word also contains specifically Platonic overtones. John Arthos (*On A Mask Presented at Ludlow-Castle* [Ann Arbor: University of Michigan Press, 1954], pp. 36–41, 62–66) discusses the Platonic doctrine of the demonic as being the realm of the spirit which is both intermediate and intermediary between the divine and the mortal. Sears Jayne ("The Subject of Milton's Ludlow Mask," in Diekhoff, pp. 184–185) cites Ficino's idea of the Platonic Daemon as the agent through which God governs and protects the lower world. For the intricacies of Neoplatonic demonology see Frances Yates, *Giordano Bruno and the Hermetic Tradition* (New York, 1969), and D. P. Walker, *Spiritual and Demonic Magic from Ficino to Campanella* (London, 1958).

[5] *1645:* l. 890; the direction occurs in all versions, with minor variations in Trinity: see the helpful table of stage directions appended to Shawcross's article in *Papers of the Bibliographical Society*, vol. 54, pp. 55–56.

[6] Eugene Haun, "An Inquiry into the Genre of *Comus*," *Essays in Honor of Walter Clyde Curry* (Nashville, 1954), p. 235.

[7] *1645:* l. 937; *Br:* l. 858; *Tr* (Fletcher Facsimile): I, 428, l. 14.

[8] *1645:* ll. 876 ff.; *Br:* ll. 788 ff. But Trinity has the direction, "to be said" (Fletcher Facsimile, I, 426, l. 9).

by th'earth-shakinge Neptunes mace,
and Tethis grave maiestick pace,
El bro: by hoarie Nereus wrincled looke,
and the Carpathian wizards hooke,
2 bro: by scalie Tritons windinge shell,
and ould sooth-sayinge Glaucus spell,
El br: by Lewcotheas lovely hands,
and her sonne that rules the strands,
2 bro: by Thetis tinsel-slippered feete,
and the songs of sirens sweete,
El br: by dead Parthenopes deare tombe,
and fayer Ligeas golden Combe,
wherwith she sitts on diamond rocks,
sleekinge her soft alluringe locks,
De: By all the Nimphes of nightly daunce,
vpon thy streames with wilie glaunce,
rise, rise, and heave thy rosie head,
from thy Corall paven bed,
and bridle in thy headlonge wave,
till thou our summons answered have,
      Listen & save.

It seems then that this section was designed to be sung, provided that the boys could do the singing.[9] Thus we have powerful evidence that the concluding portion of the masque, from the invocation of Sabrina to the end (128 lines in the acting version), was dominated by music and perhaps very largely set to music, with the result that Haun describes when he says, "If this does not make *Comus* an opera, at least it makes it operatic." [10]

[9] Henry J. Todd, in his edition, *The Poetical Works of John Milton* (London, 1801), V, 437, suggested that the first few lines of the passage may have been sung as a trio. But it seems more effective to have the passage begin and end with the voice of the Daemon; thus the brothers' voices are enclosed by and inspired by the guardian spirit.

[10] Haun, "An Inquiry into the Genre of *Comus*," p. 236. There has been a rather extensive and often highly technical debate about the extent to which *Comus* does, or does not, fit the conventions of the two genres, masque and opera. Gretchen Finney (*Musical Backgrounds for English Literature: 1580–1650* [New Brunswick, 1962], pp. 175–194), argues for the relation of *Comus* to the Italian *dramma per musica*, productions in a mixed form which combined recitative and serious plot with aspects of spectacle or masque. John Hollander (*The Untuning of the Sky: Ideas of Music in English Poetry, 1500–1700* [Princeton, 1961], p. 192), and John Demaray (*Milton and the Masque Tradition* [Cambridge, Mass., 1968], pp. 9, 146), disagree with Finney and are opposed to any attempt to relate *Comus* to the development of early opera. Wilfrid Mellers (*Harmonious Meeting: A Study of the Relationship between English Music, Poetry and Theater*, c. *1600–1900* [London, 1965], pp. 166–167) argues

Meanwhile there are clear indications of instrumental music at three points: the dances at the very close; the scene of Comus's temptation of the Lady, where the stage direction of the published version requires "soft Musick" at the outset; and the dance of Comus and his monsters near the beginning of the work, where some kind of wild music would seem to be required, for after the entering speech of Comus, the manuscripts have the stage direction: "The measure in a wild, rude, and wanton Antick." [11] In connection with the last point, one should note that the entering words of Comus are written mainly in the same swift tetrameter that is elsewhere set to or associated with music; and indeed the opening speech of Comus suggests poetry very close to the lyric form of the Anacreontic:

> Mean while welcom Joy, and Feast,
> Midnight shout, and revelry,
> Tipsie dance, and Jollity.
> Braid your Locks with rosie Twine
> Dropping odours, dropping Wine.
> Rigor now is gon to bed,
> And Advice with scrupulous head,
> Strict Age, and sowre Severity
> With their grave Saws in slumber ly.
>
> [102-110]

But shortly after this, in keeping with the loss of rigor and scrupulosity here urged, the tetrameter begins to expand into pentameter, with significant variations that ebb and flow throughout the remainder of Comus's speech, as the imagery serves to suggest:

> The Sounds, and Seas with all their finny drove
> Now to the Moon in wavering Morrice move,

that *Comus* is only superficially operatic and that many of the problems of the work are attributable to the fact that it falls between the conventions of poetry and opera. Angus Fletcher (*The Transcendental Masque: An Essay on Milton's Comus* [Ithaca, 1971], pp. 175–186) provides a very full summary of the technical debate. He also mentions the possibilities of English blank verse for spoken recitative and asserts that Milton is "a poet whose belief in his own verse was so strong that he could, if he wanted, write an opera without music, *opera senza musica*." (p. 184)

[11] *Br:* l. 164; *Tr* (Fletcher) I, 402, l. 37. The published version spoils the effect by giving simply "The Measure" (l. 144).

> And on the Tawny Sands and Shelves,
> Trip the pert Fairies and the dapper Elves.
>
> [115–118]

It is a wavering morris dance, indeed; these irregularities form a striking contrast with the strict tetrameter form that dominates the end of the masque, a regularity symbolizing the return of order to the scene, as indicated also by the dancers at the conclusion.[12] In the actual performance of the masque, this contrast would have been even more strikingly indicated by the fact that the masque opens with Lawes's song in strict tetrameter form, binding together beginning and end.

In addition to actual music, a great many allusions to and descriptions of music help to develop this theme of disorder versus harmony. The theme is stressed at the end of the "Antick" dance by Comus and his crew when Comus breaks off the "measure" with a metrical pun: "Break off, break off, I feel the different pace / Of som chast footing neer about this ground" (ll. 145– / 46). As Comus thus shifts his "footing" from tetrameter couplets to blank verse, he alerts us to the way in which music and dance merge into the music of poetry. Throughout his masque, we gradually realize, Milton is coalescing allusions to poetry, song, music, and incantation in a way represented by the Latin use of *carmen*, or by the mythical founder of all such harmonies, Orpheus.

The Lady then enters and at once reinforces the theme as she says:

> This way the noise was, if mine ear be true,
> My best guide now, me thought it was the sound
> Of Riot, and ill manag'd Merriment,
> Such as the jocond Flute, or gamesom Pipe
> Stirs up among the loose unleter'd Hinds,
> When for their teeming Flocks, and granges full
> In wanton dance they praise the bounteous *Pan*,
> And thank the gods amiss.
>
> [170–177]

---

[12] For the effect of varieties of verse form in *Comus*, see the essay by Edward Weismiller in the *Variorum Commentary*, II, 1038–1052, especially pp. 1049–1050.

The lines give perhaps some indication of the kind of music with
flute and pipe that accompanied the dance of Comus's crew. But
soon (much sooner in the acting version than in the printed
text)[13] she answers the riotous "noise" of Comus and his crew
with her own beautiful "noise," in the form of the song in which
she asks "Sweet Echo" to tell her where her brothers are, and in
the process reminds us of two myths in which suffering has been
transmuted into harmony:

> Sweet Echo, sweetest Nymph that liv'st unseen
>   Within thy airy shell
>   By slow *Meander's* margent green,
>   And in the violet imbroider'd vale
>   Where the love-lorn Nightingale
> Nightly to thee her sad Song mourneth well.

> Canst thou not tell me of a gentle Pair
>   That likest thy *Narcissus* are?
>   O if thou have
>   Hid them in som flowry Cave,
>   Tell me but where
> Sweet Queen of Parly, Daughter of the Sphear,
> So maist thou be translated to the skies,
> And give resounding grace to all Heav'ns Harmonies.

[230–243]

But the last line in the song that Lawes has set to music reads
differently and in some ways more effectively: "And hold a
Counterpoint to All Heavn's Harmonies."[14] Milton's revision
has the advantage of adding the overtones of heavenly "grace,"
but it lacks the power of the word "Counterpoint," which indeed represents the central principle of the masque: the attempt
to create, by earthly sounds and words, a melody that will work
in counterpoint with heaven's harmonies—the music of the
spheres and the music of the higher Heaven.

Here, some readers have felt, "The Lady's loneliness is en-
hanced because," contrary to our expectation, "no echo re-

---

[13] Lines 188–190 and 195–225 in the published version do not appear in Bridgewater.

[14] This is also the original reading of Trinity (see Fletcher Facsimile, I, 406,
l. 8), which is revised in accord with the printed version. Both versions of the
line thus appear to be Milton's own work. For a view of the change differing
from my own, see Hollander, *The Untuning of the Sky*, p. 322.

plies." [15] She does not receive an answer concerning her brothers, but the Lady's words to Comus at line 274 may indicate
some kind of echo:

> Not any boast of skill, but extreme shift
> How to regain my sever'd company
> Compell'd me to awake the courteous Echo
> To give me answer from her mossie Couch.

Would she refer to "courteous Echo" if Echo had not already
in some way answered her? It is hard to believe that Lawes
would have passed up a chance to perform this song with echoes,
which the pauses in the musical phrasing surely would allow.
Perhaps he himself sang the echoes.

In any case, there is counterpoint, as Comus receives the song
within himself and responds, adding another melody:

> Can any mortal mixture of Earths mould
> Breath such Divine inchanting ravishment?
> Sure somthing holy lodges in that brest,
> And with these raptures moves the vocal air
> To testifie his hidd'n residence.

> [244–248]

Comus here is forced to recognize the truth of the Pythagorean-
Platonic view of music as the emanation of the soul. Then, echoing *Romeo and Juliet*,[16] he moves toward another kind of music,
with his characteristic mutation into sensuous imagery, as of
someone's hair being stroked:

> How sweetly did they float upon the wings
> Of silence, through the empty-vaulted night

[15] *The Poems of John Milton,* ed. John Carey and Alastair Fowler (London,
1968), p. 188; Hollander, *The Untuning of the Sky,* p. 321; and the *Variorum
Commentary,* p. 891. Another interpretation of lines 274 ff. is given by C. L.
Barber ("A Mask Presented at Ludlow Castle: The Masque as Masque," in
Diekhoff, p. 200). While saying that there is no echo except in the hearing and
varied responses of Comus and Thyrsis, he argues that the Lady's strength lies
in her presumption that "she is in a world inhabited by 'courteous Presences.'"
For an extensive discussion of various verbal echoes and musical echo effects
in the poem see Angus Fletcher, pp. 198–209. Agreeing that no echo answers
the Lady, Fletcher contends that this failed response becomes, in fact, a positive sign, freeing the Lady from a narcissistic "echo chamber" to await "the true
and final echo" which is heavenly.
[16] III, ii, 18–19: Juliet's passionate wish for Romeo's presence.

At every fall smoothing the Raven doune
Of darkness till it smil'd.

And from here we move quickly into the world of Ovidian metamorphosis, where Circe and her crew put on a sort of operatic
performance all their own:

I have oft heard
My mother *Circe* with the Sirens three,
Amid'st the flowry-kirtl'd *Naiades*
Culling their Potent hearbs, and baleful drugs,
Who as they sung, would take the prison'd soul,
And lap it in *Elysium*, Scylla wept,
And chid her barking waves into attention,
And fell *Charybdis* murmur'd soft applause:
Yet they in pleasing slumber lull'd the sense,
And in sweet madness rob'd it of it self,
But such a sacred, and home-felt delight,
Such sober certainty of waking bliss
I never heard till now. Ile speak to her
And she shall be my Queen.

Then he addresses the Lady as a nature goddess, with a strong
foreshadowing of the role later to be played by Sabrina:

Hail forren wonder
Whom certain these rough shades did never breed
Unlesse the Goddes that in rurall shrine
Dwell'st here with *Pan*, or *Silvan*, by blest Song
Forbidding every bleak unkindly Fog
To touch the prosperous growth of this tall Wood.

Thus, throughout this speech, Comus is impelled to pay powerful tribute to the harmonizing effect of song that is holy, sacred,
or blessed, in contrast to the "baleful" kind of song that Comus
remembers.

Soon the two brothers enter, aged nine and eleven at the original performance; and they proceed to hold a schoolboy conversation about their sister and the power of chastity. Here is a
good example of Milton's way of creating an operatic effect
through poetry. When we watch an early opera by Monteverdi,
such as his *Orfeo*, we are aware that the interest cannot reside
in what we ordinarily call dramatic tension. The interest often

resides in watching two performers work their skillful ways through contrasting parts, each part a set piece, a show piece, designed to draw forth the utmost power of the performer's vocal skill, while evoking the essence of the character or the dilemma represented. So here, each brother is characterized by his poetry. The nine-year-old is closer to earth and natural fears; the eleven-year-old is full of superior knowledge, all out of books, able to quote Ovid and Plato to excess in order to quell his brother's fears. Thus the younger brother cries out:

> But O that haples virgin our lost sister
> Where may she wander now, whether betake her
> From the chill dew, amongst rude burrs and thistles?
> Perhaps som cold bank is her boulster now
> Or 'gainst the rugged bark of som broad Elm
> Leans her unpillow'd head fraught with sad fears.
> What if in wild amazement, and affright,
> Or while we speak within the direfull grasp
> Of Savage hunger, or of Savage heat?
>
> [350–358]

And the elder brother replies with a highly condescending tone:

> Peace brother, be not over-exquisite
> To cast the fashion of uncertain evils;
> For grant they be so, while they rest unknown,
> What need a man forestall his date of grief,
> And run to meet what he would most avoid?
>
> [359–363]

But when the younger brother has the temerity to continue with his fear that some "ill greeting touch" may harm his sister, the elder brother answers with an even more supercilious tone in the following interchange:

> My sister is not so defenceless left
> As you imagine, she has a hidden strength
> Which you remember not.
> *2 Bro.* What hidden strength,
> Unless the strength of Heav'n, if you mean that?
> *Eld. Bro.* I mean that too, but yet a hidden strength
> Which if Heav'n gave it, may be term'd her own:
> 'Tis chastity, my brother, chastity.
>
> [414–420]

I do not see how any audience, particularly the original audience, could do anything but smile at this encounter: the whole scene could, and should, I think, be acted or imagined in such a way as to create something of the effect of a school play on Parents' Day. Certainly the elder brother's command of the situation is put in serious doubt when he declares:

> So dear to Heav'n is saintly chastity,
> That when a soul is found sincerely so,
> A thousand liveried Angels lacky her,
> Driving far off each thing of sin and guilt.
>
> [454–457]

However excellent the elder brother's knowledge of Plato is, we have just seen the Lady walking off the stage with Comus. But there is at least one liveried spirit to protect her, and he now enters at line 490, garbed as the shepherd Thyrsis.

We are bound to recall that Thyrsis was the singer in the first Idyll of Theocritus who sang the famous lament for Daphnis; but the present shepherd's power of song is not left to implication. The elder brother addresses Thyrsis with a musical compliment:

> *Thyrsis?* Whose artful strains have oft delaid
> The huddling brook to hear his madrigal,
> And sweetn'd every muskrose of the dale,
> How cam'st thou here good Swain?
>
> [494–497]

These words echo the Spirit's own words at the end of his prologue, where he says:

> But first I must put off
> These my skie robes spun out of *Iris* Wooff,
> And take the Weeds and likenes of a Swain,
> That to the service of this house belongs,
> Who with his soft Pipe, and smooth-dittied Song,
> Well knows to still the wilde winds when they roar,
> And hush the waving Woods.
>
> [82–88]

Here too the audience might display a quiet smile, for the Spirit is here speaking the poet's compliment to Henry Lawes, while

Lawes himself pays Milton's own tribute to the poet's smooth ditties! Both of these descriptions evoke another archetype of poet and musician—Orpheus, who had this power over nature, but could not subdue the destructive powers of the Bacchantes —and Comus is the son of Bacchus, we must recall. The myth and the entire tradition of Orphic religion are central to the action of *Comus*.[17]

Appropriately, then, Thyrsis now describes the Miltonic myth of Comus's birth as son of Bacchus and Circe (ll. 520– 523), a passage followed by a memory of the "monstrous rout" we have just heard "doing abhorred rites to *Hecate*" (ll. 532– 536). And now, beginning at line 540, Thyrsis proceeds to develop what we might call a poetical aria on the basic theme of this masque. First he describes how he sat on a bank (reminiscent of *Midsummer Night's Dream*) "to meditate my rural minstrelsie," and how he then heard the "wonted roar" and "barbarous dissonance" that we ourselves have seen and heard enacted before us:

> At which I ceas't, and listen'd them a while.
> Till an unusuall stop of sudden silence
> Gave respit to the drowsie flighted steeds
> That draw the litter of close-curtain'd sleep.
> At last a soft and solemn breathing sound
> Rose like a steam of rich distill'd Perfumes,
> And stole upon the Air, that even Silence
> Was took e'er she was ware, and wish't she might
> Deny her nature, and be never more
> Still to be so displac't.
>
> [551–560]

It is of course the Lady's song which we have just heard; and we are struck now with the contrast between Comus's reception of that song within his mind and the less sensuous, more spiritual manner of the Spirit's reception:

---

[17] On the idea of Orpheus during the late Middle Ages and Renaissance and on Orphic ritual and incantation see Yates, *Giordano Bruno*, pp. 78–80 and 89–91; and D. P. Walker, "Orpheus the Theologian and the Renaissance Platonists," *Journal of the Warburg and Courtauld Institutes*, 16 (1953), 100–120. Numerous readers have noted the analogy with Orpheus, especially Angus Fletcher (*The Transcendental Masque*, p. 168), who also treats the description in lines 86–88 as indicating the "Orphic powers" of the Attendant Spirit. See also his mention of the Lady's powers as an "Orphic voice" on pp. 170 and 173 and his discussion of the Orphic voice of the poem on pp. 186–91.

> I was all eare,
> And took in strains that might create a soul
> Under the ribs of Death.
>
> [560–562]

Shortly after this the Spirit tells the two brothers of the charm that he bears against enchantments of Comus's kind, in a passage that requires the closest examination, because it seems to have something to do with music and poetry:

> Care and utmost shifts
> How to secure the Lady from surprisal,
> Brought to my mind a certain Shepherd Lad
> Of small regard to see to, yet well skill'd
> In every vertuous plant and healing herb
> That spreds her verdant leaf to th'morning ray,
> He lov'd me well, and oft would beg me sing,
> Which when I did, he on the tender grass
> Would sit, and hearken even to extasie,
> And in requitall ope his leather'n scrip,
> And shew me simples of a thousand names
> Telling their strange and vigorous faculties;
> Amongst the rest a small unsightly root,
> But of divine effect, he cull'd me out;
> The leaf was darkish, and had prickles on it,
> But in another Countrey, as he said,
> Bore a bright golden flowre, but not in this soyl:
> Unknown, and like esteem'd, and the dull swayn
> Treads on it daily with his clouted shoon,
> And yet more med'cinal is it then that *Moly*
> That *Hermes* once to wise Ulysses gave;
> He call'd it *Haemony*, and gave it me,
> And bad me keep it as of sov'ran use
> 'Gainst all inchantments, mildew blast, or damp
> Or gastly furies apparition.
>
> [617–641]

None of the explanations of that mysterious herb, Haemony, wholly satisfies me. I would like to suggest another explanation, which will probably satisfy no one but myself. But I am encouraged to continue after reading recently a summary of the controversy given by Woodhouse in the new *Variorum Commentary*:

It must be confessed that each of the explanations here reported or suggested presents some difficulty. . . . It is difficult to see how moral doctrine can itself protect; and if for doctrine one substitutes the moral quality or saving influence which the doctrine enjoins or describes, it is not in the power of a second person to bestow it— whether one interprets the quality as temperance (which leaves unexplained the clear differentiation of Haemony from Moly) or the influence as grace (which raises the new difficulties of the evident limitation upon the power of Haemony and the whole relation to the Sabrina episode). Finally, the explanation last offered above, while it meets the other difficulties, leaves the name Haemony unexplained and obviates none of the difficulty respecting the Shepherd Lad. The reader may perhaps conclude that the crux has not been completely resolved and be content to await further light.[18]

Hanford long ago suggested that the shepherd lad might represent Milton himself, the young poet, admiring Lawes's music.[19] From this standpoint the various "simples" given to Thyrsis from the Lad's "scrip" would be poems, and the small unsightly root might be the image of poetic inspiration—poetry being an art not esteemed in England and hence not flourishing, but in Greece or Italy (or in Heaven) of great beauty and effect. Can the name Haemony bear this interpretation? One should remember that the Greek word *haimon* means *skillful*, and we have just heard the shepherd lad described as "well skill'd." At the same time the word seems to derive from Haemonia, an ancient name for Thessaly, land of magical herbs, as Milton himself regards it in his *Elegy II*, where he refers to the rejuvenation of Aeson by Medea as told by Ovid in the *Metamorphoses* (7. 251–293). We should recall, too, that Haemonia is the region of Greece that contains the Vale of Tempe, consecrated to pastoral poetry. Furthermore, among the many references to this region of Haemonia in Ovid, my friend John Pope has pointed out to me the possible significance of one allusion in Ovid's *Remedia Amoris*: "If anyone thinks that the baneful herbs of Haemonia and arts of magic can avail, let him take his own risk. That is the old way of witchcraft; my patron Apollo gives harmless aid in sacred

[18] *Variorum Commentary*, II, 937. For a summary of the numerous allegorical interpretations of *haemony* see the *Variorum*, pp. 932–938. An addition to the literature since the appearance of the *Variorum* is Sacvan Bercovitch, "Milton's 'Haemony': Knowledge and Belief," *Huntington Library Quarterly*, 33 (1970), 351–359.
[19] James Holly Hanford, *A Milton Handbook* (New York, 1954), pp. 159–60.

song." [20] Of course, the remedies for lust that Ovid then proceeds to provide are hardly those that Milton recommends; but
it would be characteristic of Milton to revamp the Ovidian suggestion in his own way. Is it then "sacred song" that gives one
the power to penetrate disguises, guard from evil, and rescue
from enchantment?

It seems so, for when the brothers fail to rescue the Lady,
through their inexperience, the Attendant Spirit himself moves
to the rescue through poetical (musical) means:

> Som other means I have which may be us'd,
> Which once of *Meliboeus* old I learnt
> The soothest Shepherd that ere pip't on plains.

(The heavy alliteration serves to identify the shepherd as Edmund Spenser.)

> There is a gentle Nymph not farr from hence,
> That with moist curb sways the smooth Severn stream,
> *Sabrina* is her name, a Virgin pure . . .
> And, as the old Swain said, she can unlock
> The clasping charm, and thaw the numming spell,
> If she be right invok't in warbled Song,
> For maid'nhood she loves, and will be swift
> To aid a Virgin, such as was her self
> In hard besetting need, this will I try
> And adde the power of som adjuring verse.
>
> [821–826, 852–858]

Then follows the operatic conclusion to the poem in which song,
dance, and orchestral music serve to create a harmony in which
the oppositions of life are reconciled, and nature and spirit are
brought into a rich union represented by Sabrina's song:

> By the rushy-fringed bank,
> Where grows the Willow and the Osier dank,
>   My sliding Chariot stayes,
> Thick set with Agat, and the azurn sheen
> Of Turkis blew, and Emerauld green
>   That in the channell strayes,

[20] *Remedia Amoris*, ll. 249–252, in the translation by J. H. Mozley, Loeb Library, *Ovid*, II. The passage is also cited by Angus Fletcher, *The Transcendental Masque* (p. 194), for a different purpose.

Whilst from off the waters fleet
Thus I set my printless feet
O're the Cowslips Velvet head,
  That bends not as I tread,
Gentle swain at thy request
  I am here.

[890–901]

Indeed, the more we ponder the work, the sounder Gretchen
Finney's basic argument appears to be: that the masque, as Milton developed it, resembles the form that opera was beginning
to take in the early part of the seventeenth century.[21] To see the
work as thus related to opera may help to resolve some of our
critical problems. The operatic analogy seems to be the best way
of answering the usual criticism of the work, as put by Samuel
Johnson, who complained that the speeches "have not the sprite-
liness of a dialogue animated by reciprocal contention, but seem
rather declamations deliberately composed and formally repeated on a moral question. The auditor therefore listens as to a
lecture, without passion, without anxiety." From this point of
view, Johnson contends: "The dispute between the Lady and
Comus is the most animated and affecting scene of the drama,
and wants nothing but a brisker reciprocation of objections and
replies, to invite attention and detain it." [22]

But if we listen operatically, we will not seek a brisker reciprocation, which would prevent the greatest delight of opera:
the listening, with passion, to an aria deliberately composed and
formally repeated by a skillful performer. From this standpoint
Comus's great aria of temptation is a showpiece designed to
outdo all previous exhortations of the *carpe diem* kind, including
Thomas Randolph's recent Cavalier piece;[23] while the Lady's
answer, strengthened by Milton's addition in the published version (ll. 778–805), provides her with a worthy response, as she
utters her own operatic climax:

Thou art not fit to hear thy self convinc't
Yet should I try, the uncontrouled worth

---

21 See the work by Gretchen Finney cited above, n. 10.
22 Samuel Johnson, *Lives of the English Poets*, ed. G. B. Hill, 3 vols. (London,
1906), I, 119-120.
23 For the passage from Thomas Randolph's *The Muses Looking Glasse*
frequently cited as an analogue to Comus's temptation speech, see the *Variorum
Commentary*, II, 773-775.

Of this pure cause would kindle my rap't spirits
To such a flame of sacred vehemence,
That dumb things would be moved to sympathize,
And the brute Earth would lend her nerves, and shake,
Till all thy magick structures rear'd so high,
Were shatter'd into heaps o're thy false head.

[792–799]

Thus the Lady proves to have a power of eloquence that defeats the sensual music of Comus.[24] "She fables not," Comus admits to himself; "I feel that I do fear / Her words set off by som superior power" (ll. 800–801).

Milton's masque, then, is an exhibition of the music of poetry such as only John Milton could have given at this particular point in his career. It is a feast of nectared sweets performed with all the arts that Milton has now mastered from various models. It is a poem that displays a mastery of the blank verse of Shakespeare and the Jacobean drama. It displays a mastery of the art of madrigal and air. It displays to perfection the Jonsonian mode of couplet-rhetoric, especially in the form of the tetrameter. It echoes the whole range of Elizabethan and Jacobean dramatic productions, from the *Old Wives' Tale* to the latest masques by Thomas Carew and Aurelian Townshend.[25] It displays the prologue of the supernatural agent derived from Euripides, along with the stichomythic dialogue of the Greek drama. It can draw upon the whole range of pastoral poetry from Theocritus to Spenser. It is indeed a virtuoso display of poetical mastery, with the young Milton, at the age of twenty-five, showing himself now almost ready to embark upon the great work for which he has been so carefully preparing his powers.

For us today Milton's masque must have its value, I believe, in its demonstration of Milton's vital belief in the power of poetry and music, in its demonstration that the harmonies of art can overcome the wiles of evil. I do not mean to say that we should

[24] See the excellent essay by Philip Brockbank, "The Measure of 'Comus,'" *Essays and Studies*, 21 (1968), 46–61, for a fine discussion of three kinds of "verbal music" in Milton's masque: the "sensual music" of Comus, the "moral music" of the elder brother, and a third kind represented in the Lady's song: "a Miltonic song quite distinct from the sensual music and the moral music, and yet related to both: a transfigured and sublimated sensuality." For this, Brockbank finds the apt term, "Hesperian music" (pp. 55–58).

[25] For extensive discussion of the relationship of *Comus* to the masque tradition, and to *Tempe Restored* in particular, see Demaray, *Milton and the Masque Tradition*, pp. 59–96.

ignore the many studies that have shown the depth and subtlety
of Milton's moral and religious themes in the masque. But we
should not lose sight of the fact that Milton's simple plot, like
his whole volume of 1645, is designed to show a progress toward
maturity.[26] I believe that too much ink has been spent upon the
question of whether Milton really believes that chastity is equal
to charity. After all it is not Milton who utters that famous substitution;[27] it is a young lady of fifteen who does not yet understand, as Sabrina does, that charity must complete the role of
chastity. Sabrina combines the spirit of music with the spirit of
charity and evokes throughout the countryside, not the riotous
noise that the Lady has feared to meet in her earlier speech, but
rather the music of a virtuous pastoral festival:

> still she retains
> Her maid'n gentlenes, and oft at Eeve
> Visits the herds along the twilight meadows,
> Helping all urchin blasts, and ill luck signes
> That the shrewd medling Elfe delights to make,
> Which she with pretious viold liquors heals.
> For which the Shepherds at their festivals
> Carrol her goodnes lowd in rustick layes,
> And throw sweet garland wreaths into her stream
> Of pancies, pinks, and gaudy Daffadils.
>
> [842–851]

The spirit of music which the Lady has revealed in her opening song shows that she has within herself a richer nature than
her philosophic speeches to Comus can reveal. Like Sabrina, she
will live to fulfill that promise, until her own shepherds, at their
festivals, will "Carrol her goodnes lowd in rustick layes."

BIBLIOGRAPHICAL NOTE

A facsimile of the Bridgewater manuscript (115 lines shorter
than the printed version), with transcription, is available in *John*

---

[26] For an excellent treatment of the work from this standpoint, see Gale H.
Carrithers, Jr., "Milton's Ludlow *Mask:* from Chaos to Community," *ELH*,
33 (1966), 23–42.

[27] See the *Variorum Commentary*, II, 805–808, 828–829, 845–846, for a quite
full summary of the debate over Milton's substitution in lines 213–216, of the
triad Faith, Hope, and *Chastity*, for Faith, Hope, and *Charity*.

Milton's Complete Poetical Works Reproduced in Photographic Facsimile, edited by Harris Francis Fletcher, 4 volumes (Urbana, 1943–1948), I, 300–339. Fletcher's transcription is reprinted, with useful textual notes, in the indispensable collection edited by John S. Diekhoff: *A Maske at Ludlow: Essays on Milton's Comus* (Cleveland, 1968), pp. 207–240. My citations of Bridgewater (*Br*) are taken from Diekhoff.

Henry Lawes's autograph manuscript of the songs is on deposit in the British Library and is available from the library as Microfilm PS7/10980. (See Coburn Gum, "Lawes Folio," *Milton Newsletter*, 3 [March, 1969], 4–5.) Willa M. Evans (*Henry Lawes: Musician and Friend of Poets* [New York, 1941], p. 102) provides a facsimile of "From the Heav'ns" taken from this manuscript. A second manuscript, Br. Mus. Add. MSS 11518, is thought to be an eighteenth-century transcript of the autograph: see Andrew J. Sabol, *Songs and Dances for the Stuart Masque* (Providence, 1959), page 167; Sabol bases his transcription on this manuscript, which is reproduced in the Fletcher Facsimile, I, 340–344. Other printed versions of Lawes's music follow the collation of the two musical manuscripts done by Hubert J. Foss for *The Mask of Comus*, edited by E. H. Visiak (Bloomsbury: The Nonesuch Press, 1937). Foss's version is reprinted in *The Masque of Comus*, edited by Mark Van Doren and H. Foss (Cambridge, [1957]); and also in Diekhoff, pages 241–250.

A facsimile of the Trinity College manuscript, with a transcription by William Aldis Wright, is available in the Fletcher Facsimile, I, 383–455. A handy and inexpensive facsimile of the Trinity MS, also with Wright's transcription, has been published by the Scolar Press, 1972.

Unless otherwise noted, my citations of the text of *Comus* are based on the edition of the 1645 text in *The Poetical Works of John Milton*, edited by H. C. Beeching (Oxford, 1904). For the purposes of this article, I refer simply to the "published version" and cite the text as *1645* without differentiating between the editions of 1637 and 1645.

For full discussion of the chronology and various revisions of the texts see: John S. Diekhoff, "The Text of *Comus*, 1634 to 1645," in *A Mask at Ludlow*, ed. Diekhoff, pp. 251–275; *A Variorum Commentary on the Poems of John Milton*, by A. S. P. Woodhouse and Douglas Bush (New York, 1972), II, 735–740; John T. Shawcross, "Certain Relationships of the Manuscripts of

Comus," *Papers of the Bibliographical Society of America,* 54 (1960), 38–56, and "Henry Lawes's Settings of Songs for Milton's 'Comus,' " *Journal of the Rutgers University Library,* 28 (1964), 22–28. After this essay was sent to press, another important contribution to the textual study of *Comus* appeared: *A Maske: The Earlier Versions,* ed. S. E. Sprott (Toronto, 1973). It contains a detailed and sound study of the manuscripts, and it prints the versions of Trinity, Bridgewater, and 1637 in parallel columns.

I am indebted to Louise Brown Kennedy for extensive assistance in the preparation of the notes to this essay.

VI

PROBLEM SOLVING IN COMUS

Stanley E. Fish

Comus criticism is pre-eminently a criticism of problems. Here, for example, is B. A. Rajan's report on just one of the disputes that has grown up around Milton's masque:

The confrontation between the Lady and Comus seems to be set in a dark wood of critical disagreement. The most popular view is that the Lady wins largely by refusing to lose and that Comus walks off with the forensic and poetic honors. Other suggestions are that the Lady is right but not the Elder Brother, that both the Lady and Comus are wrong and the epilogue right, that nobody and nothing is right except the whole poem and even that the whole poem seems to have gone wrong somewhere.[1]

The question here is, who is right, the Lady or Comus? but it cannot be asked without asking a series of other questions. Is the Lady, as Comus claims, a stoic? In what sense, if any, are we obligated to nature? When does temperance become the "lean and sallow abstinence" (l. 709)? What are the terms "By which all mortal frailty must subsist" (l. 686)? What exactly is the "sage / And serious doctrine of Virginity" (ll. 786–787)? And if we turn to other parts of the masque, the questions multiply: Why do the brothers leave their sister? Why is the Lady taken in by

[1] "*Comus:* The Inglorious Likeness," *University of Toronto Quarterly,* XXXVII, no. 2 (1968), 121.

Comus's disguise? Is she in any way tempted by what he offers? Is she safe, as the Elder Brother declares, or is she, as the Younger Brother insists, "single and helpless," vulnerable to the "rash hand of bold Incontinence" (l. 397)? What is Haemony? Who is Sabrina? Why are the brothers and the Attendant Spirit unable to free the Lady? Whose "glutinous heat" (l. 918) besmears the seat on which she sits? With whom, if anyone, are we to identify Adonis, Venus, Cupid, Psyche? And as if these questions were not enough, the mask ends with an implied question:

> Mortals that would follow me,
> Love virtue, she alone is free
> She can teach you how to climb
> Higher than the Sphery chime;
> Or if Virtue feeble were,
> Heav'n itself would stoop to her.
>
> [1018–1023]

Well, is virtue feeble or is she not? The verse forces the question, but the poet, like Bacon's jesting Pilate, does not stay for an answer.

The critics, of course, have stayed, but the answers they give do not, on the whole, satisfy. I do not intend to offer my own set of answers, but to suggest that we pay more attention to the questions, that is, to the pattern of their asking and to the pattern of response their asking creates. For if the criticism proves anything, it is that questioning is the activity to which *Comus* moves us, and therefore it seems reasonable to regard the questions we are moved to ask as primary data, rather than as loose ends that are to be tied up as neatly and quickly as possible.

As a first step in that direction let me point out that there are even more questions than the critics have recognized; for in addition to those posed directly and urgently by the events of the narrative, there are those that surface only for the moment it takes to read or listen to a word or a line. Consider, for example, the introductory speech by the Attendant Spirit:

> Before the starry threshold of *Jove's* Court
> My mansion is, where those immortal shapes
> Of bright aerial Spirits live inspher'd
> In Regions mild of calm and serene Air,
> Above the smoke and stir of this dim spot,

Which men call Earth, and with low-thoughted care
Confin'd and pester'd in this pinfold here,
Strive to keep up a frail and Feverish being,
Unmindful of the crown that Virtue gives
After this mortal change, to her true Servants
Amongst the enthron'd gods on Sainted seats.
Yet some there be that by due steps aspire
To lay their just hands on that Golden Key
That opes the Palace of Eternity:
To such my errand is, and but for such,
I would not soil these pure Ambrosial weeds
With the rank vapours of this Sin-worn mould.

[1–17]

These seventeen lines firmly establish a two-tiered Platonic universe and they also establish an opposition between the freedom and expansiveness of the higher tier and the closeness and constraint of the level to which the spirit descends. Earth is a "dim spot," a "pinfold" (enclosure for animals); its inhabitants are frail and feverish; they are confined and restricted, both in their physical circumstances and in their point of view; they are prisoners of a "Sin-worn" mold which the Attendant Spirit most uncharitably disdains to assume.

In the next line, however, the language and the system of value it reflects suddenly change (the Attendant Spirit is still speaking):

But to my task. *Neptune,* besides the sway
Of every salt Flood, and each ebbing Stream,
Took in by lot 'twixt high and nether *Jove,*
Imperial rule of all the Sea-girt Isles
That like to rich and various gems inlay
The unadorned bosom of the Deep;
Which he to grace his tributary gods
By course commits to several government,
And gives them leave to wear their Sapphire crowns,
And wield their little tridents; but this Isle,
The greatest and the best of all the main,
He quarters to his blue-hair'd deities;
And all this tract that fronts the falling Sun
A noble Peer of mickle trust and power
Has in his charge, with temper'd awe to guide
An old and haughty Nation proud in Arms:
Where his fair off-spring nurs't in Princely lore,

> Are coming to attend their Father's state,
> And new-entrusted Sceptre.
>
> [18–36]

The perspective is still one that looks downward from aery heights to spotlike enclosures, but the colors have changed from the gray and brown of smoke and mold to the richly various colors of sapphire and other gems inlaid in the blue bosom of the sea; and the inhabitants of these spots, one of whom is "greatest" and "best," are no longer low-thoughted or feverish or rank, but noble, powerful, tempered, and fair.

There is of course a simple explanation for this apparent contradiction: presumably neither Milton nor Lawes would wish to insult the Earl of Bridgewater by suggesting that he and the members of his family were sinful, much less odorous;[2] obviously they are among those few that "by due steps aspire" to be free of their earthly prison. I do not want to belittle this explanation, but it would be difficult to extend it to the subsequent instances of the same pattern; for repeatedly the verse invites us to adopt an attitude toward some thing or person or action only to turn in a few lines and apparently sanction exactly the opposite attitude. This is true even of those objects and places which, as Roger Wilkenfeld has shown, "establish the masque's concern with the varieties of restraint and confinement:"[3] pinfolds, spots, prisons, dungeons, cells, caves, cages, caverns, grots, sties, snares, traps, vaults, sepulchers, graves, every kind of enclosure imaginable, including the verbal enclosures of "well placed words of glozing courtesy" (l. 161) and "false rules prankt in reason's garb" (l. 758). Chief among these is the enclosure of "the drear wood" in whose "perplex't paths" the Lady and her brothers wander. This wood is "ominous" (l. 61), thick with "black shades" where hidden dangers lurk "imbow'red"; it is "a wild wood" (l. 312), a "close dungeon" (l. 349), a "surrounding waste" (l. 403), a "dark sequestr'd nook" (l. 500), a "hideous wood" (l. 520), the "haunt" of sorcerers who are "Immur'd in cypress shades" (l. 521), a place of "inmost bow'rs" (l. 536), where a monstrous rout like "stabled wolves" (l. 534) can be heard howling. Yet at

---

[2] Especially in the light of the evidence uncovered by Barbara Breasted in "Comus and the Castlehaven Scandal," in Milton Studies III, ed. J. D. Simmonds (Pittsburg, 1971), pp. 201–224.

[3] "The Seat at the Center: An Interpretation of Comus," ELH, XXXIII (1966), 174.

times these same woods wear a quite different face; if they are
"ominous" when the Attendant Spirit speaks of them at line 61,
they are friendly, or at least sympathetic, at line 86, when he recalls how they cease their waving in response to the "soft pipe
and smooth dittied song" of Thyrsis. In one breath the Lady
complains of her confinement in "the blind mazes of this tangl'd
wood" (l. 181), and in the next she remembers how inviting
these woods seemed only a short time ago, when "the spreading
favor of these Pines" offered lodging and shade. Even now, in
the midst of her danger, she refers to the "kind hospitable
Woods" (l. 187) which provide berries and other cooling fruits.
Of course the balance remains negative; the wood continues to
be the prime symbol of the menace of enclosure; but then enclosures are themselves not always perceived as menacing. As the
Younger Brother debates the degree of his sister's danger, he is
conscious of his own, lost and imprisoned in "this close dungeon
of innumerous boughs" (l. 349); but when he turns for solace to
an image, it is of an enclosure no less confining than the one he
would escape: "might we but hear / The Folded flocks penn'd in
their wattled cotes" (ll. 343–344). If danger is a dungeon, then
safety, it would seem, is a cage, and when the Elder Brother asks
"hath any ram / Slipt from the fold, or young Kid lost his dam,
/ Or straggling wether the pent flock forsook?" (ll. 497–499),
safety is again strongly equated with confinement.

What are we to make of this? Are some enclosures good and
others bad? Are the same enclosures now good, now bad? In
some cases it is possible to account for the discrepancy by reference to the plot. When the Lady calls the wood "kind and hospitable" she merely displays the vulnerability that will soon lead
her to say to Comus, "Shepherd I take thy word, / And trust thy
honest offer'd courtesy" (ll. 322–323). To solve the problem in
this way, however, is only to confront a larger one. Why is it
that the good characters in the masque seem so much at a dis-
advantage? The Lady is the victim not only of Comus's rhetoric,
but of Milton's irony. She calls to Echo and asks for grace; she
is heard by Comus and delivered up unto the enemy. While her
soon-to-be-tempter addresses her in a curious and suspect mixture of overcourtly and overpastoral diction, she responds with
platitudes about the likely residence of true courtesy, and
blithely cries, "Shepherd lead on." Her brothers fare no better.
Their lapse, excusable or not, leads directly to the crisis, and
their performance in the climactic scene is no more happy, as the

Attendant Spirit is quick to point out: "O ye mistook, ye should have snatcht his wand / And bound him fast; without his rod revers't / And backward mutters of dissevering power, / We can not free the Lady that sits here / In stony fetters fixt, and motionless" (ll. 815–819). Not that the Spirit himself is notably successful; he was dispatched, he tells us, for "defense and guard" (l. 42), but he is always appearing a moment after the damage has been done, and whatever Haemony is, his possession of it does not enable him to free the Lady.

I am not suggesting that we are confused as to who is good and who is bad; indeed, it is precisely because we are *not* confused that the unfolding of the masque presents us with a succession of problems; for given the certain knowledge that the Lady deserves our sympathy and admiration, while Comus does not, we are pressed in the course of reading or viewing to find objective correlatives for that certain knowledge. The conservative critics[4] are surely right when they insist that the theme of *Comus* is simply the superiority of virtue over vice; but in our experience of the masque that theme is apprehended negatively, because for so much of the time we are learning wherein the superiority of virtue does *not* reside. It does not reside in physical strength, nor in invulnerability, nor in infallibility; it does not even reside, as we discover, in a delicacy of perception. When the Lady appears on the scene, her first words are "This way the noise was, if mine ear be true" (l. 170), and in fact her ear *is* true, for she correctly assesses the nature of Comus's rites even though she has not like us had the advantage of seeing them. (This impressive performance should be a sufficient answer to those who see in this speech the fastidiousness of a prig.) If we are tempted, however, to generalize from this to an assertion of the superior trueness of virtuous ears, we are stopped short by the example of Comus himself, who in the very same scene displays an ear no less true: "Can any mixture of Earth's mold / Breathe such Divine enchanting ravishment? / Sure something holy lodges in that breast" (ll. 244–246). Indeed, as it turns out Comus finally has the best of this comparison, as he does of

[4] In this group I include among others Robert M. Adams, *Ikon: John Milton and the Modern Critics* (Ithaca, 1955), pp. 1–34; Marjorie Nicholson, *John Milton: A Reader's Guide to his Poetry* (New York, 1963), pp. 67–86; A. E. Dyson, "The Interpretation of *Comus*," *Essays and Studies*, n.s., VIII (1955), 89–114.

others; for while he draws the correct conclusion from the Lady's voice, she is disastrously mistaken about his: "Shepherd, I take thy word." Of course Comus is disguised, the Lady is not, and as Rosemond Tuve points out, virtue does not enable one "to see through to the true nature of that which . . . simply says it is other than it is." [5] Here then is a firm point of difference between virtue and vice; one is open, the other works by guile. This distinction, however, holds up no better than the others. The Attendant Spirit also works by guile; he too disguises himself as a shepherd, and the putting on of his disguise is the first action we see. Indeed since they never appear on stage at the same time, the Attendant Spirit and Comus could be played by a single actor.

To this one might object that while the Attendant Spirit and Comus perform identical actions, their intentions differ, and that difference is essential. Yes it is, but notice how we have come to that conclusion (I assume you, reader, as an interlocutor)—by entertaining more immediately available points of difference and then discarding them because they prove to be *in*essential. This, I believe, is precisely what we are doing (or should be doing) when we read *Comus*, learning to perceive essential differences in the context of surface similarities. That is to say, reading (or viewing) the masque is like performing a rough and ready feature analysis in the course of which we discover what something is by first discovering what it is not. We are provoked to this discovery by the apparent lack of fit between the characters (as they are labeled) and what they do or say; but this lack of fit exists only if value is thought to be a property of things or actions (that is, of words and disguises), and it is precisely that way of thinking that the masque is designed to change. In short, I am suggesting that the problems posed by the masque are *heuristic;* they are there not because we are to solve them, but because we are to be provoked by them to a certain kind of activity, the activity of getting something straight.

This is precisely the activity in which the Elder and Younger Brothers are engaged, and indeed, their conversation should be seen as either a model or a parody of the dialogue taking place in our minds. The point of debate between them is exactly the

[5] "Image, Form and Theme in *A Mask*," in *Images and Themes in Five Poems by Milton* (Cambridge, Mass., 1957), p. 128.

point at issue in our experience as readers or viewers, not whether the Lady is virtuous (that is assumed), but the nature and shape of her virtue; and they proceed as we do, by progressively refining their idea of what is essential. They begin on the smaller (but related) issue of whether or not the Lady is in danger, and the Elder Brother weighs in immediately with a generalization: "Virtue could see to do what virtue would / By her own radiant light, though Sun and Moon / Were in the flat Sea sunk . . . / He that has light within his own clear breast / May sit i'th' center and enjoy bright day" (ll. 373–375; 381–382). To this ringing declaration, the Younger Brother replies with a common-sense objection: "You may as well spread out the unsunn'd heaps / Of Miser's treasure by an outlaw's den, / And tell me it is safe, as bid me hope / Danger will wink on Opportunity, / And let a single helpless maiden pass" (ll. 398–402). It might appear at this point that the Elder Brother begins to give ground, but what he does is define more precisely the ground on which he continues to stand. That is, he *uses* his brother's objections, much as we are to use the discontinuities we perceive, to make finer and finer discriminations. It is not, he declares, our sister's physical strength in which I have confidence, but "a hidden strength / Which you remember not" (ll. 415–416). And what is that, the Younger Brother obligingly asks (how like a Platonic dialogue this is) and he is immediately told: " 'Tis chastity, my brother, chastity: / She that has that, is clad in complete steel / . . . no evil thing that walks by night / . . . Hath hurtful power o'er true virginity" (ll. 420–421; 432; 437). This raises the question of what is meant by *true* virginity, a question that is answered when Thyrsis arrives with news of the Lady's capture. Since the audience already knows what has happened, much of his speech is redundant; but its function is less to give information than to generate a pressure for the further zeroing in on the subject. Again, the Younger Brother takes the role of foil or prod: "Is this the confidence / You gave me, Brother?" (ll. 583–584). And the reply is so sure that it begins on the half line, without missing a beat:

>   Yes, and keep it still,
> Lean on it safely, not a period
> Shall be unsaid for me: against the threats
> Of malice or of sorcery, or that power
> Which erring men call Chance, this I hold firm;
> Virtue may be assail'd, but never hurt,

Surpris'd by unjust force, but not enthrall'd,
Yea even that which mischief meant most harm
Shall in th' happy trial prove most glory.

[584–591]

In this passage the process of refining is accelerated, every line contributing to the further specifying of the Elder Brother's position and therefore of the conceptions that support it. To the earlier distinction between external and internal strength, he now adds a series of distinctions: virtue may be attacked (this is after all a comment on the attacker), but the attack will prove unsuccessful; of course it may *appear* successful in some merely physical sense ("Surpris'd by unjust force"), but that appearance will only serve finally to make virtue's inevitable triumph more dramatically satisfying; for in the end "evil on itself shall back recoil, / And mix no more with goodness" (ll. 593–594).

I am aware that my summary of these lines is selective, but I believe that my selection is true to the rhythm of the exchange, which is dialectical, moving from a consideration of relative strength and weakness, to the redefining of strength as an interior rather than a physical quality, to the identification of that quality as chastity, to the redefining of chastity as something (not yet specified) that can survive a bodily assault, even if, in some superficial way, that assault is successful. In short, what the brothers do, in cooperation, not in conflict, is separate accidents from essentials, and since that is what we have been doing all along, their activities parallel and interact with ours. It follows, then, that we are not on one side of an argument, but on both sides of a process, exploring with the brothers the contrasting perspectives on their sister's situation. Thus when the Younger Brother expresses fear that the Lady may be in real danger, we know that he is right, and for that moment at least, he is, in his questioning, our surrogate; yet when the Elder Brother declares that the truly virtuous are dear to Heaven and are therefore under the protection of angels, we know that *he* is right, because we have seen and heard the angel who protects his sister. The critics treat this scene as if at the end of it we were to award the palm to one of the speakers, but this is to ignore its dialectical movement and the answering movement it draws from us. The brothers are not adversaries (except on local issues of interpretation), but partners, with each other and with us, and our common goal, at least in that part of the scene that has been called "philosophical," is the goal of every philosopher, to find out what really matters, to get something straight.

And meanwhile, what of the Lady? What is she doing while her brothers philosophize and we proceed with them toward an identification of essentials? She is not trying to get something straight, for she has it straight already. While her brothers labor for three hundred lines to understand the extent and limits of her danger, and while we exercise our minds no less strenuously (if less formally), she articulates the crucial distinction within moments of her first appearance. After acknowledging (1) that she is lost, (2) that she is possibly in danger, and (3) that she is surely in the neighborhood of evil spirits (these are precisely the points the Younger Brother will later make), she declares simply: "These thoughts may startle well, but not astound / The virtuous mind" (ll. 210–211). If I were to paraphrase this, I could do no better than the Elder Brother's statement of lines 588 ff.: "This I hold firm; / Virtue may be assail'd but never hurt. . . ." The point of course is that the Lady is holding firm from the very beginning, aware, as her brothers are, of the possibility that she may be "surprised by unjust force"—that is, "startled"—but knowing before they do (or at least before they articulate it) that such an assault cannot shake an inner composure which is based on a faith in something more real than the accidents of physical circumstance. The virtuous mind, in short, may be temporarily put off balance by something totally unexpected, but it will always recover itself and refuse to be paralyzed (*astounded*). The fact that the Lady will later be literally paralyzed is only one more indication of the extent to which the meaning of events is not discernible in their observable configurations.

Meanwhile, however, we are still left with our question, more sharply focused: if the Lady is not in the process of getting something straight, what is she doing? The answer is, that she is gradually being placed in a position where the basis of the confidence she here displays is plainly visible, because every other basis for it has been taken away. Even before she appears on the scene, she has been stripped of the support provided by her brothers; and in rapid succession she is stripped of all the supports that remain: the stars are, as she says, "closed up" and no lamp is available to "give due light / To the misled and lonely Traveller" (ll. 199–200); she then turns to her ear, "my best guide now" (l. 171), and for a while it serves her well as she discerns perfectly the quality of the sounds she hears; but then Comus appears with his well-placed words of glozing courtesy and what had been her "best guide" now points her in exactly the wrong direction: "Shepherd, I take thy word, / And trust thy honest offer'd courtesy." Friends, light, vision, hearing, direction, one by one they are taken from her, until in Comus's lair she is deprived even of her mobility and is left with nothing at all.

Yet, as it turns out, she is left with everything—*that matters.* This is what is meant when she says to Comus "Thou canst not touch the freedom of my mind" (l. 663), or, in other words, "all of this—my weakness, your strength, the entire situation as it seems to be—is beside the point. I may be imprisoned in every sense you can conceive, but in truth I am free." The force of this moment (if it is felt) inheres in the way it reverses yet maintains the opposition in the opening lines between the constraint of earthly pinfolds and the freedom of those who sit on sainted seats. The Lady is obviously one who "by due steps" aspires to sainthood, and yet she sits here a virtual emblem of the confinement associated by the Attendant Spirit with feverish worldly striving. Here, then, is another problem for the audience, but it is solved even as it is (literally) posed if we realize that a distinction originally made in terms of place is here redefined as a distinction of spirit: from the point of view of the physical circumstances the Lady is helpless, defenseless, and "immanacl'd" (l. 665); from a point of view that denies the primacy of the physical, she is formidable, protected, and free. It is this hierarchy of perspectives that the scene establishes, or rather asks us to establish by asking us to understand what the Lady says. The careers of the audience and the heroine are thus perfectly complementary: she begins with layers of support, but they gradually fall away, leaving her to rely on what is essential; we begin with an understanding of virtue, but it is gradually refined by our efforts, until at some point we identify what is essential. Her moment of trial (or, more properly, of self-exemplification) requires an affirmation, and we are required to comprehend it; the text for both is the same:

Thou canst not touch the freedom of my mind.

This, then, is the act (of understanding) for which the heuristic experience of the masque has been preparing us, and if we perform it, the problems that were the vehicle of that experience disappear, not because they are solved, but because they have been made meaningful. That is, the distinction we are invited to make here—between a vantage point from which the Younger Brother's fears are justified and another from which they are irrelevant—operates retroactively to turn the questions that have led us to make it into answers, Is the earth a pinfold or a gem? Are the woods ominous or kind? Are disguises good or bad? The form of these questions is "either-or" but the answer in every case is "both-and": the earth is both a pinfold and a gem, depending on whether you are tied to it by "low-thoughted care" or live, at least in spirit, in "Regions mild of calm and serene Air"; the woods are both ominous and kind, depending on whether Comus or some superior power is believed to be their proprietor; disguises are both good and bad, depending on the purpose for which they are put on; and of course the Lady is both secure and in danger, depending on whether one fears for her physical well-being or for the integrity of her mind and soul. No one of the questions raised by the masque is to be answered unequivocally, although it is the search for unequivocal answers that brings us to this realization. The pattern of ambiguous valuing exerts a pressure for resolution and explanation (for getting something straight), but when the explanation is found, it does not disambiguate. Rather, it gives significance to the pattern by establishing contexts in which the interpretive alternatives are simultaneously, but not indifferently, true. Once these contexts have been established, every event and image in the masque falls into place as a further exemplification of the only lesson it teaches, the lesson of the double perspective.

So powerful is this lesson that at a stroke it does away with the critical puzzles associated with *Comus*, not by making them disappear, but by making them signify. Consider, for example, the most notorious of these problems. What exactly is Haemony? Temperance, reason, faith, knowledge, general grace, specific grace, prevenient grace, full grace, partial grace, anticipatory grace? The question has a literature of its own,[6] and I have no intention of adding to it, except to ask another question. What are we told about Haemony? Only that it is a "small unsightly root," the leaf "darkish" and "prickled," but that in "another country" it bears a "bright golden flow'r"; not, however, "in this soil: where it is unknown" and unesteemed and "the dull swain / Treads on it daily with his clouted shoon" (ll. 634–635). In short

---

[6] See on this point *A Variorum Commentary on the Poems of John Milton,* Volume Two (Part Three), ed. A. S. P. Woodhouse and Douglas Bush (New York, 1972), pp. 932–938.

Haemony is something that is weak and unimpressive from one point of view, but strong and glorious from another, precisely the distinction we have learned to make between virtue as it appears in earthly terms, and virtue as it is seen and valued in Heaven. I am not suggesting that Haemony is virtue, but that they both figure forth or fill out the double perspective which is at once the subject of the masque and the goal of our refined understandings. The critics have erred in seeking to assign a different significance to each of the masque's abstractions, for this is to assume a casual or sequential relationship between the components of the action, whereas in fact, the relation is between successive manifestations of a single great image or controlling idea. The plot of *Comus* is not a series of crises (although several scenes have that appearance), but of transformations; and the pleasure we derive is, as Rosemond Tuve has said, "the pleasure of watching the central image unfold, display itself, dance before us . . . The image which is the heart of this frail action slowly opens out one meaning after another, never disappearing, never standing still, looking at us with one face out of the long and leisurely speech of one stylized personage, with another face out of the songs and declarations of another, is seen in this position and in that" (ll. 154–155). Haemony then does not signify something *different* from the actions or symbols presented elsewhere in the masque; rather it is one more face of the meaning that is continually exfoliating, the meaning I have identified as the double perspective, or the pattern of ambiguous valuing, or, more colloquially, the principle of "it is and it isn't." The Lady's situation, fixed but free, is an emblem of that principle; Haemony, unsightly but beautiful, is another.

The famous temptation scene is another still; for the debate between Comus and the Lady is not to be watched with suspense (will she or won't she) or with a view toward judging the arguments, but as one more context for the unfolding of the points of view we have learned to distinguish. Thus Comus's position is perfectly coherent given his assumption that man is bound to the processes of nature; for then the obligation he urges is indeed paramount and the Lady's abstinence is what he says it is, a self-glorying asceticism that would deny her involvement in the "condition / By which all mortal frailty must subsist" (ll. 685–686). The Lady, as many have observed, replies not by answering him, but by *declaring* another position, one in which his offer and her behavior take on quite a different appearance: in her vision, all mortal frailty subsists by virtue of the sustaining power of God, and Nature is only an intermediary bestower of that sustenance; therefore to bind oneself to Nature in the manner Comus suggests is to set her up in place of God, and in fact to do her a disservice by placing her in a configuration of choice in which she is an idol. Temperance in this view is not the negative and constricting thing Comus takes it to be, but the sign of a refusal to be in bondage to natural processes and a declaration of dependence on a power that controls, and can at any time suspend, them. Temperance, then, is a positive and liberating action, and it takes its place with Haemony as something that signifies differently, depending on where you stand, just as Nature takes its place alongside earth, and the wood, and pinfolds, as something whose value is a function of your relationship to it, a prison if you allow yourself to be confined within its confines, a temple if as you move within it you continually "look to Heav'n" (l. 777).

Together, then, the two positions in the debate form another instance in a continually exfoliating pattern of paired antitheses: the Lady's apparent situation is to her true situation as the unimpressive appearance of Haemony is to its true beauty and efficacy, as the superficial negativity of temperance is to its liberating intention, as the ominous woods are to the woods that are kind, as the disguise of Comus is to the disguise of the Attendant Spirit, as the enchanting song of Circe is to the holy song of the Lady's waking bliss, as the Nature that demands our worship is to the Nature that calls us to the worship of God. What makes these opposing pairs equivalent and even interchangeable is the larger opposition in which they participate and of which they are manifestations: on one hand a perspective that values on the basis of appearances and on the other a perspective in which value is a function of a hierarchy of loyalties. These perspectives are, as we have seen, present and distinguished in the opening lines, and the events of the plot serve only to confirm the previously chosen allegiances of the characters. Just as there is no progression in the action, so there is no advance in the level of insight displayed by the villain and heroine who merely reaffirm and redefine the positions from which they always speak. For all its dramatic impact, the Lady's ringing "Thou canst not touch the freedom of my mind" is nothing more (or less) than a reformulation of her earlier declaration of a mind that can be startled but not astounded, and this in turn anticipates the Elder Brother's confident faith in a virtue that can be surprised but not enthralled. In each of these statements the interpretive center is shifted from the realm of physical accident to the realm of spiritual essence, and an ethic of intention is substituted for an ethic of observable effects. That ethic received yet another formulation (and we receive yet another opportunity to understand) when the Lady refuses Comus's offer of a "cordial julep" (l. 672):

> Were it a draught for *Juno* when she banquets,
> I would not taste thy treasonous offer; none
> But such as are good men can give good things.
>
> [701-703]

This is the furthest (and inevitable) extension of the truth the masque continually presents. If virtue is a function of motives or loyalties, then it cannot be identified with things or actions, which are neither good nor bad in themselves but take on the moral coloration of those who use and perform them. The categories "good things" and "good actions" are determined by the spirit in which they are appropriated and executed. The Lady is not good because she does X; rather, X is good because *she* does it. And exactly the reverse is true of the actions and offers of Comus, which are intended (by Milton) less to persuade than to supply the other pole of the two world views the masque is always contrasting.[7]

Comus, then, is essentially static (a description that many have turned into a criticism) but its experience is not; for, as Rosemond Tuve observes, although the "clearly opposed . . . positions do not conflict in any stage personality . . . we ourselves are that personality" (l. 121). What this means is that the events of the mask are always serving a double purpose: they measure, from a variety of angles, the distance between the two contrasting perspectives, and they invite the audience to perceive that distance and to understand its implications. Nowhere is the distance greater or the invitation more pressing than when the Lady

[7] As William Madsen has observed ("The Idea of Nature in Milton's Poetry" in *Three Studies of the Renaissance* [New Haven, 1958]), this position is central to the Platonic-Augustinian tradition that finds a classic expression in Augustine's *On Christian Doctrine*. There "the important question is . . . Whom do you love? If like Comus, you love yourself and your own pleasure, you are a member of the City of Babylon; if you like the Lady, you love God . . . you are a member of the Heavenly City of Jerusalem" (p. 204). It is these two perspectives, these alternative loyalties, that are figured forth in the actions and statements of the characters who do not merely hold different points of view, but live in different universes.

declines to expound "the sage / And serious doctrine of Virginity" (ll. 786–787):

> Fain would I something say, but to what end?
> Thou hast nor Ear nor Soul to apprehend
> The sublime notion and high mystery
> That must be utter'd to unfold the sage
> And serious doctrine of Virginity.

[783–787]

This too is a point of critical debate that has a literature of its own, but like Haemony the sage and serious doctrine is a problem only if one wishes to assign it a separate meaning, for in fact it is identical with the stable meaning every event and image presents. The virginity celebrated here (even though it is unexpressed) is the virginity of the virtuous soul that refuses to ally itself with terrestrial values and is pledged instead to the higher power of which all things terrestrial are evidences. It is this pledge and self-betrothal (to something not seen) that Comus is incapable of understanding, and the Lady proves *her* understanding (rather than her arrogance or ignorance) by not trying to explain it to him. What she leaves out, we are left to supply, performing an overt act that is precisely answerable to her act of omission. "List mortals, if your ears be true," cries the Attendant Spirit in the Epilogue (997); it is my thesis that *Comus* is a device for the making true of its audience's ears, which are here tested, as they have been tested before, by their ability to understand.

They are tested once more as the masque ends: "Mortals that would follow me, / Love virtue, she alone is free, / She can teach ye how to climb / Higher than the Sphery chime, / Or if Virtue feeble were, / Heav'n itself would stoop to her." You will recall that this was one of the first of the questions I posed at the beginning of this essay. Is virtue feeble or is she not? It is hardly even necessary to answer, "she is and she isn't." She is in the sense that external circumstances are beyond her control; she isn't in the sense that the measure of her strength is the firmness of the will. That is why the appearance of Sabrina is only contingently related to the efforts of the brothers and the steadfastness of the Lady; not, as some have suggested, to protect the freedom of grace, but to underline the freedom of virtue which is as independent (in its own sphere) of heavenly intervention as it is immovable before the lure of earthly temptations. Sabrina, the last of the problems for which criticism has sought a solution, is, like everything else in the mask, not an isolated value, but a second term in a relationship that helps us to further refine our understanding of virtuous behavior. In a curious way, she is allied with Comus, for both function as foils to the Lady who remains the center of an attention they serve to focus. It is as wrong to make the nymph the heroine of the action as it is to make a hero of the tempter. *Comus* is no more a celebration of grace than of nature. Rather, it is a celebration of human virtue, of her limited glory and glorious limitations.

I conclude as I began, with the criticism, for it has been my intention here to reconcile critical camps by transforming their disagreement into an insight about the way the poetry works. The disagreement is between the conservative critics who tell us to read the major scenes in the context of Platonic-Christian doctrines, and the critics of the "ingenious" party who cry "what about this" and "you've ignored that." What I have been arguing is that "this" and "that" (the problems of my title) are there precisely so that we will become capable of reading the mask just as the conservative critics tell us it should be read. Thus while there is no real movement in the action, except for the overdetermined movement of opposites reassuming their opposing positions in a variety of postures, there is (or should be) movement in the understandings of the spectators. As Stephen Orgel has observed, "it is not the Lady, but we ourselves who . . . come away with a lesson for our lives." [8] Learning that lesson (of the double perspective) is the activity to which the masque calls us; watching it repeated in a triumphant succession of exfoliations is the pleasure it offers. That pleasure is not transitory, for to enjoy it here is to have become capable of enjoying it when the performance is over and we move from the interpretive trials of art to the interpretive trials of living. The purpose of a masque, Orgel tells us (borrowing from Jonson), is "to make the spectators understanders." In the course of understanding the Lady's virtue, we earn a share of it, becoming what we apprehend. The spirit that has been the key to every one of the masque's problems informs the reader or viewer who has learned to proceed in its light. In short, the reward for reading *Comus* properly is not merely comprehension or even instruction, but conversion.

[8] *The Jonsonian Masque* (Cambridge, Mass., 1965), p. 153.

INDEX

Authors, titles (under author's name when known), and a few subjects are included. The forematter of this book sets forth its authors and their topics.

133